ENGAGING THE ORGANIZATION IN EFFECTIVE PERFORMANCE MANAGEMENT

Translating Vision into Results

Dr. Richard T. Beck

Mr. John L. O'Brien

Disclaimer and Terms of Use Agreement

Table of Contents

PREFACE: Engaging the Organization in Fulfilling a Vision 1

Chapter 1: Guiding Principles...5

    Principle #1 - Facilitate involvement across the organization.........................7

    Principle #2 - Exercise active rather than passive management 9

    Principle #3 - Realize where less can be more 11

    Key points 14

Chapter 2: Developing a Strategic Plan Using a Combined Top-down/Bottom-up Approach 16

    Strategic Plan components..16

    Combined top-down/bottom-up strategic planning.....................................23

    Employing a Strategic Plan Framework..25

    Review: Steps for creating a Strategic Plan..27

    Key points 29

Chapter 3: Determining Strategic Goals and Strategic Objectives.....................30

    Determining Strategic Goals...30

    Determining Strategic Objectives 35

    Key points 37

Chapter 4: Designing Performance Measures..38

    Design Characteristic #1: Able to reliably count a commodity or effect produced due to the organization's actions..39

    Design Characteristic #2: Recognized as meaningful/useful by leadership, workforce, stakeholders, and constituents 43

    Design Characteristic #3: Applied/tracked routinely in practice..................47

Design Characteristic #4: Measurable at a reasonable cost 48

Design Characteristic #5: Possess a verifiable approach of measurement ... 49

Key points..50

Chapter 5: Performance Assessment Techniques.............................52

Routine plan vs. actual tracking 52

Red/Yellow/Green assessments 56

Comparing performance and funding trends over multiple years 60

Conducting routine performance status reviews 66

Key Points 70

Chapter 6: Using Performance Information for Budget Formulation 72

Navigating the government budget formulation process....................72

Tools for performance-informed budget planning 76

Organize budget decisions into three tiers....................................81

Tier 1: Baseline Budget - Maintaining existing approved programs.............83

Tier 2: Augmentations to existing programs 85

Tier 3: New Initiatives and Opportunities 85

Creating budget justifications...86

Key points..87

Chapter 7: Agency Priority Goals – Targeting Specific Areas for Success........89

Operational Description..89

Routine Status Reviews 91

Key points..92

Chapter 8: Organizational Considerations for Effective Performance
Management 94

Senior leadership 94

Senior management 95

Organization-wide performance analysts 96

Specialized technical experts 99

Administrative, management, and technical support............99

Key points 100

Chapter 9: Summary - Is This All Worth It? What's Next?.......... 101

Review of tools... 101

Is This All Worth It? 102

What's Next?... 103

Appendix A: Single Program Area Trend Analysis 106

Appendix B: Multiple Program Area Analysis - Scatterplot............ 109

Appendix C: Performance Management Analyst Competencies.......... 118

REFERENCES... 124

SUPPLEMENTAL RESOURCES 126

PREFACE: Engaging the Organization in Fulfilling a Vision

How can you better ensure your organization's success? We believe that employing performance management can help improve an organization's ability to achieve results. Some may see performance management in only negative terms of identifying deficiencies, issuing punitive actions, and generating reports. However, when applied appropriately it can be much more. Performance management can help connect executives and the technical workforce in a positive way to better ensure achievement of the vision established for the organization.

In this book, the term "performance management" encompasses strategic planning, performance measurement, and corresponding analyses for assisting decision-making and helping the organization's effectiveness. This book provides instruction on how to install performance management practices in an organization to help:

- translate vision into a set of implementable strategic goals and objectives;
- align technical capabilities to help better inform and achieve the organization's vision;
- track progress to improve the probability for successfully achieving that vision; and
- engage the organization's workforce in helping realize the vision.

We present a comprehensive approach for linking the organizational vision with the means for better ensuring its realization using many of the planning and performance practices of the Government Performance and Results Act (GPRA) Modernization Act (GPRA-MA; Public Law 111-352). By addressing the development of an organization's strategic plan including vision statement, mission statement, strategic goals, and strategic objectives, we examine why the performance of an organization should be measured. It is our contention that a comprehensive strategic planning/performance measurement culture can facilitate senior leadership and management decision-making and achieving organizational outcomes.

Organizations that apply these practices should do so in accordance with three guiding principles described in Chapter 1. These guiding principles have been found to enhance collaboration and motivation across the organization. They are based on research and practical experience in designing, establishing, and conducting processes that have helped senior leaders and managers oversee and guide their government organizations. Background research includes the author's doctoral study on fostering collaboration and innovation across organizational units (Beck, 1993), findings published in academic journals (e.g., Public Administration Review, Public Performance Management Review), and reports from the IBM Center for the Business of Government, and the Center for American Progress. These findings have been used by the authors in designing and leading budget formulation processes for 23 years at NASA and performance management processes for 14 years across the Department of the Interior; and providing instruction at the National Defense University (17 years), Office of Personnel Management's Eastern Management Development Center (6 years), and George Mason University (5 years).

Topics found in the book's nine chapters are outlined as follows:

Chapter 1: Guiding Principles for Effective Organizational Performance Management

Based on the authors' research and experience, three guiding principles are essential to conducting effective performance management:

- Facilitate involvement across the organization;
- Exercise active rather than passive management; and
- Realize where less can be more.

These principles are especially important for improving the organization's collaboration and motivation among its workforce to help achieve the mission goals established by the organization's leadership.

Chapter 2: Developing a Strategic Plan Using a Combined Top-down/Bottom-up Approach

Employing a combined top-down/bottom-up approach is important to creating an effective organization. This chapter will describe strategic plan development, the relative roles of leadership and the technical workforce, and the nature of their interactions. Employing a Strategic Plan Framework can help define the organization's strategic goals and objectives in alignment with its technical capabilities.

Chapter 3: Determining Strategic Goals and Strategic Objectives

Clearly defined strategic goals and strategic objectives have a critical role in coordinating the means for accomplishing an organization's mission and improving the probability of success. Determining these strategic goals and objectives, and how to align them with the organization's resources and processes, will be illustrated.

Chapter 4: Designing Performance Measures

The characteristics of government performance measurement will be discussed, along with procedures for creating effective performance measures, types of performance measures, challenges of measuring government performance, and guarding against potential misinterpretation and frustrations.

Chapter 5: Performance Assessment Techniques

The application of performance assessment techniques will be described along with their strengths and weaknesses. These include routine plan vs. actual tracking, red/yellow/green assessments, and comparing performance and funding trends over multiple years. Effectively conducting performance status reviews using the results from these assessments will also be discussed.

Chapter 6: Using Performance Information for Budget Formulation

The means for effectively using performance information to help determine and justify budgets is examined along with a three-tier process for deciding upon the content of the organization's budget proposal. A more detailed discussion of how the performance and funding trend analyses can be employed are presented in the appendices.

Chapter 7: Agency Priority Goals – Targeting Specific Areas for Success

Highlighting certain goals with a specific target and timeframe bring added attention and collaboration to areas of particular importance. These specific goals can help energize an organization in implementing a specific change and/or taking corrective actions.

Chapter 8: Organizational Considerations for Effective Performance Management

The various roles and skills needed to ensure effective strategic planning and performance measurement are discussed, along with some organizational structure considerations.

Chapter 9: Summary - Is This All Worth It? What's Next?

This chapter provides the "forest for the trees" perspective to help the reader review the tools that have been presented throughout the book. A flow chart recaps the steps for implementing a performance management system including corresponding participants and estimated timeframes.

Reference and supplemental reading materials are provided at the end of this book .

Chapter 1: Guiding Principles

To be effective, the performance management processes presented in this book should be implemented in the context of the following three guiding principles:

- Principle #1 - Facilitate involvement across the organization;
- Principle #2 - Exercise active rather than passive management; and
- Principle #3 - Realize where less can be more.

These principles were developed through academic research and practical experience facilitating decision-making and managing federal government agencies. Background research includes the author's doctoral study on fostering collaboration and innovation across organizational units (Beck, 1993), findings published in academic journals (e.g., Public Administration Review, Public Performance Management Review), and reports from the IBM Center for the Business of Government, and the Center for American Progress. These findings have been used by the authors in designing and leading budget formulation processes for 23 years at the National Aeronautics and Space Administration (NASA) and performance management processes for 14 years across the Department of the Interior; and providing instruction at the National Defense University (17 years), Office of Personnel Management's Eastern Management Development Center (6 years), and George Mason University (5 years).

Principle #1 for facilitating involvement across the organization was gleaned from the author's doctoral research (Beck, 1993). His findings provided evidence that directly involving technical personnel across related organizational units facilitated collaboration and innovation among participants. These findings were subsequently reaffirmed when applied to the successful development of organization-wide processes used in government agencies including the following:

- an integrated program office approach for converging military and civilian weather satellite systems under the Clinton Administration's National Performance Review;
- a full cost management approach which led to successful achievement of budget and performance integration under the Bush Administration's President's Management Agenda;
- a three-tier executive budget decision process; and
- planning and performance measurement processes for the Department of the Interior.

The benefits of Principle #2 on active management are supported by research and experiences where performance is actively discussed rather than only passively published in a report. Research indicates that performance measures are more likely to be used in decision-making when they are considered useful by the technical manager and the executive (Kamensky, 1993 and Lu, 2008). Quarterly status reviews with direct involvement of senior leadership, management, and technical workforce have been found to increase the use of performance information (Government Accountability Office, 2018). Similarly, performance "stat" reviews have shown positive results in helping achieve success, likely due to actively involving leadership and managers in direct discussion of performance information. For example, New York City Police Department CompStat meetings compared crime related factors and results across precincts to determine best practices.

Principle #3, on realizing where less can be more, is based on reactions to the voluminous performance reporting of the late 1990's into the early 2000's, recommendations from a Senate subcommittee hearing on the use of performance information, and the success of applying Agency Priority Goals. An AGA (Association of Government Accountants) report from 2006 titled, PAR: The Report We Hate to Love, claimed that for all of their information, government performance and accountability reports (PAR) had limited use and recommended, "…[they] should focus on a few key metrics." In a Senate subcommittee hearing (2009) on the use of performance information, witnesses testified that government performance activity had focused more on complying with reporting requirements than analyzing and acting on performance information. They proposed that a reduced number of more strategically-oriented measurable goals would improve the use of performance information.

Subsequent to the hearing, Agency Priority Goals (to be discussed later in Chapter 7) were created. We have witnessed where senior leadership and management were more willing to review and discuss performance information when it involved a limited number of goals of their particular interest. Some federal agencies decreased the number of goals and performance measures in their Strategic Plans, providing a more focused, easier-to-digest strategic summary-level perspective of their aspirations and progress (also see guidance from the Office of Management and Budget, 2010).

We believe employing strategic planning and performance management within the context of these three principles can lead to a more collaborative and potentially productive working environment. This includes senior leadership and management synchronizing their vision with the technical knowledge and implementation skills of the organization. Such an alignment helps improve the likelihood of achieving the vision. In providing its input, the technical workforce are drawn further into helping achieve the goals that were developed for realizing the vision defined for the organization.

Principle #1 - Facilitate involvement across the organization

Involving the organization's technical workforce with the visionary and strategic decision-making of senior leadership and management can be beneficial to an organization's success. For involving the organization's technical workforce, it is important for senior leadership and management to:

- familiarize the technical workforce with the organization leadership's vision, philosophies, and goals;

- help the technical workforce understand how their contributions fit into achieving the organization's goals and success;
- increase direct involvement of the technical workforce in defining the organization's goals and objectives; and
- encourage individuals to find and develop direct working relationships, even if across organizational boundaries, to better ensure success.

One of the most effective motivations for members of the workforce is the desire to contribute, i.e., to exercise one's technical expertise and skill to help the organization succeed. To activate that motivation, it is up to the organization's executives to provide opportunities that involve the technical workforce in contributing their expertise to define and review progress toward achieving the organization's goals. This also helps ensure the technical viability of the plans that are developed for the organization, improving the probability for realizing the corresponding vision.

KEY CONCEPT: One of the most effective motivations for members of the workforce is the desire to contribute. To activate that motivation, it is up to the organization's executives to provide opportunities that involve the technical workforce in contributing their expertise to define and review progress toward achieving the organization's goals.

In applying Principle #1, senior leadership and management should also be involved in the routine review of performance toward achieving the organization's goals. Their involvement helps them better understand the technical challenges that could impede progress and the potential for success. In being directly informed, senior leadership and management can assess the potential impact to other parts of the organization and/or any possible political backlash. They can provide assistance that is outside the reach of the individual program (e.g., added funding, agreement to a modified schedule, help identify and secure partners, etc.). More importantly, senior leadership and management's involvement indicates their continued endorsement of the program despite its problems, and their willingness to help find a solution. This provides positive encouragement to the technical workforce and their continued efforts.

Principle #2 - Exercise active rather than passive management

Active management involves productive discussions among members of senior leadership, management, and the technical workforce, often leading to decisions that determine an organization's performance. In the Senate subcommittee hearing (2009) mentioned earlier, participants discussed ways to improve the actual use of performance information beyond merely complying with documentation requirements. More direct discussion of performance information among senior leadership, management, and technical workforce was considered necessary. In these discussions, senior leadership, management, and technical workforce would apply their corresponding perspectives to interpreting the results of performance analyses and jointly, collaboratively decide how to proceed and better achieve results. Such active discussions on performance information have been applied effectively through performance "stat" reviews (also see Keegan, 2015) and quarterly status reviews.

As opposed to active management, passive management is typified by producing required documentation that is rarely, if ever, used in decision-making that effects an organization's outcomes. Signs of passive management include processes that produce documentation that is:

- primarily published or posted with limited interested consumers;
- used by only a limited set of individuals who may provide observations but do not affect a decision or achieving results;
- rarely referenced in meetings, discussions, collaborations, or decision-making within the organization; and
- perceived as lacking value by senior leadership and management.

The processes presented in this book are designed to help apply Principle #2, facilitating a more active management approach, rather than producing large downloads of data or reams of pages in a document. These processes are presented in a manner to promote interaction among senior leadership, management, and technical workforce for finding the best solution to a problem or challenge.

KEY CONCEPT: Gathering performance data must go beyond a "check the box" exercise. Performance information must be used in actual strategic decision-making.

Implementing active management under Principle #2 goes hand-in-hand with Principle #1 of organizational involvement discussed earlier. Active management gives the leader, manager, and technician a means by which each can infuse their own individual skills and talents directly into the organization's problem-solving and decision-making. This direct interaction helps more individuals see themselves as contributors to the organization's success, validating the value of their role in the organization's efforts, and providing a sense of ownership in the organization's results. From organization theorists Henri Fayol (1916), Luther Gulick (1937), and Herbert Simon (1976) we understand that organizations can benefit from dividing work among groups of individuals with specialized skills. Rather than having each member of the workforce work on all aspects of a program, dividing up the program's tasks among groups of the appropriately skilled specialized experts can be more effective. The organization's senior leadership and management bring the contributions of these specialized groups together. Practicing active management helps ensure these skills are effectively coordinated and applied to helping the organization achieve results.

Principle #3 - Realize where less can be more

Employing too many details can become confusing and delay the ability to reach a decision. The more details that are provided, the more time and effort is needed to sort through the details, determine which details are most useful to making the decision, and assessing the options. At the organizational level, where numerous programs, projects, and functions contribute to achieving a strategic objective or goal, the quantity of available details can be staggering. Therefore, senior leadership and management need a more structured strategic decision process where the quantity of details is streamlined to those most useful to making the decision. These selected details need to be organized to facilitate understanding and assessing the various options. This streamlining of details needs to be accomplished in a way that provides information rather than just data points that leads to an effective decision.

From Charles Lindblom (1959), we noticed that decision-making can be incremental where any significant decision is divided up into smaller partial decisions spread out over time. Each partial decision would then be made based on the experience following the prior partial decision. In designing the means for modeling social and natural systems to increase understanding, Jay Forrester (1968) employed a select set of key relationships and factors considered most relevant to determining a result. Forrester's simulation models do not necessarily replicate the details of reality; their value is in improving understanding. Both Lindblom's and Forrester's solutions appear to involve a more selective use of details. Along with the increased use of performance information by senior leadership and management that was observed by professional performance staff when using fewer Agency Priority Goals, we have come to recognize that less can be more.

In accordance with Principle #3, the level of detail being presented for decision-making should match the corresponding level of management. An organization's senior leadership and management's perspective is oriented more across the scope of the organization's components and guiding achievement of the overall mission than trying to accommodate the depth of details from all the components. Senior leadership and management are more likely to engage in the use of performance information when the information is streamlined to suit their strategic role. Similarly, external stakeholders might be more satisfied and supportive when they are provided overarching perspectives related to mission achievement rather than too many implementation details.

As the pyramid in Figure 1 depicts, there is an increasing quantity of details in the various programs/projects and support functions depicted toward the wider base of the pyramid. These programs/projects and support functions conduct the full range of work that achieve the strategic goals and objectives. There are typically fewer goals and objectives near the top of the pyramid, as they combine the contributions from the more numerous programs/projects and support functions toward achieving the mission.

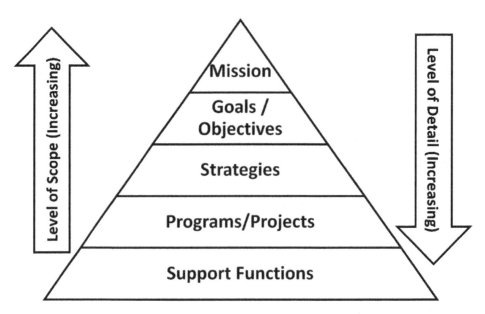

Figure 1. Match the level of detail to the corresponding level of management

At the top of the pyramid, senior leadership and management need to determine if all the contributing components throughout the scope of the organization are progressing effectively toward achieving the mission. However, trying to consider the full range of details across all of the contributing components would be overwhelming. The sheer number of details can take much time and effort to sort through.

Selecting the most relevant data for senior leadership and management to consider, and setting aside the more ancillary data, can provide focus. With a more selective set of information, senior leadership and management can make their assessment at the organization level, and notify the appropriate program/project manager or technical staff in the lower levels of the pyramid where corrective action is needed. The program/project managers and technical staff at the lower levels of the pyramid are in a better position to deal with the numerous implementation details in each of their particular areas. In this way, the level of detail is matched with the corresponding level of management.

KEY CONCEPT: Match the level of detail to the corresponding level of management.

Using key performance indicators can help streamline the quantity of details to be considered at the upper levels of leadership and management. Key performance indicators are designed to provide a more summarized representation of conditions and progress across the organization. If further detail is needed beyond that provided by the key performance indicators, there can always be targeted follow-up discussion scheduled with the corresponding collection of specialized experts. The application of certain graphics, including bar charts, pie charts, line graphs, and scatterplots, can also help provide perspective while using a streamlined set of data (to be discussed further in Chapter 5 on Performance Assessment Techniques).

Under Principle #3, we believe that the organization's senior leadership and management, who do not have the time to sort through an expansive collection of details, are more likely to use performance information provided with a less cluttered approach. Their use of the performance information can encourage the corresponding use of performance information by the technical workforce. As discussed with Principles #1 and #2 for involving the technical workforce and active management, senior leadership and management working directly with the technical workforce can help improve the organization's probabilities for success. Therefore, the senior leadership and management should not be burdened with too many of the vast amount of implementation details that may have limited utility in making decisions that determine the organization's success. In your own organization, consider if all of the performance details being reported are actually used in decision-making. Or are the details provided just because they exist? Remember that a more effective discussion of performance information among senior leadership, management, and technical workforce for decision-making can be facilitated by using less rather than more.

Key points

- To be effective, the performance management processes presented in this book should be implemented in the context of three guiding principles:
  - o Principle #1 - Facilitate involvement across the organization.
  - o Principle #2 - Exercise active rather than passive management.
  - o Principle #3 - Realize where less can be more.
- Facilitating involvement across the organization can help motivate its technical workforce in pursuing the vision established for the organization. One of the most effective motivations for members of the workforce is the desire to contribute.

- Exercising active management facilitates problem-solving by connecting leadership's visionary interests with the expertise of the technical workforce to help better ensure the practicality for achieving results.
- Realizing where less can be more can help ensure continued involvement of both leadership and the technical workforce in measuring performance and achieving results. Match the level of detail with the corresponding level of management. Reducing the clutter of too much data can help better focus attention on finding the right solution.

Chapter 2: Developing a Strategic Plan Using a Combined Top-down/Bottom-up Approach

The Government Performance and Results Act (GPRA) Modernization Act of 2010 (GPRA-MA) requires federal agencies to produce a Strategic Plan every four years with the following key components:

- a comprehensive Mission Statement
- strategic goals and objectives
- a description of how the goals and objectives are to be achieved (i.e., strategy)

It is from this legislation that we find the language of strategic planning. Contained in this piece of public policy is the terminology for the components of performance management. All government leaders should become familiar with such topics as vision statements, mission statements, strategic goals, strategic objectives, and strategies.

Strategic Plan components

A Strategic Plan conveys the overarching vision for the organization, its purpose (i.e., mission), and corresponding activities for realizing the vision. As reflected in Figure 2, the mission statement provides the overall purpose of the organization, the goals reflect what the organization is trying to achieve, while the strategic objectives specify what the organization will do to achieve its goals. For each strategic objective, key performance indicators are used to track how much progress is being made in implementing each of the strategic objectives toward reaching the goal. Strategic initiatives include the implementation details for achieving the objectives, with project-level performance metrics to measure progress.

The idea of defining vision, mission, and goals is to ensure that the organization's operations, defined by the strategic objectives and initiatives, are aligned with its strategic direction, so that all activities pull in the same desired direction. A strategic goal is an elaboration of the vision and mission statement. An organization's strategic goals should provide greater specificity of the desired future (or end state) that the organization is working to achieve.

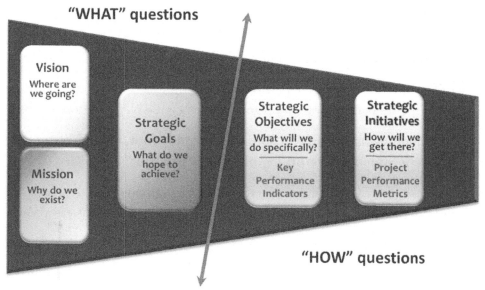

Figure 2. Strategic plan components define the "what" and "how" for the organization.

Vision Statement

Every organization should have a vision statement. An organization's vision should provide a vivid description of what the organization wants to become. Vision statements should offer a tangible and compelling image of a highly challenging but achievable direction for the organization. A good vision statement:

- represents consensus concerning what the organization can become
- provides a beacon; giving organizational members direction
- is brief, communicates in simple language
- challenges and inspires organizational members to put forth their best efforts

Some of the common attributes of a good vision statement include the following:

- shows where the organization is going in the future
- inspires and energizes the workforce
- helps create a mental image of the idealized state
- a statement for the organization to rally around

One of the most dramatic examples of an inspiring vision statement is the one given by President Kennedy in 1961 concerning the NASA moon mission:

"…achieving the goal, before this decade is out, of landing a man on the moon and returning him safely to earth."

This statement had a major impact on the country's consciousness. It galvanized NASA, industry, and the United States citizenry to focus efforts at that audacious goal.

Mission Statement

For the organization's leadership, the Strategic Plan is an opportunity to convey their vision for the organization's purpose in a mission statement and corresponding goals. A mission statement gives the purpose of the organization, its reason for being. A mission statement is often derived from mandates and includes the larger social or political needs that the organization seeks to fill.

A good mission statement:

- states why your organization exists
- describes what your organization does
- states what outcomes you are attempting to create for your customer
- provides guidance for strategic and operational decision-making to get the whole organization focused to meet the customers' needs

Some of the common attributes of a good mission statement include the following:

- defines success
- achievable
- measurable
- results-oriented
- identifies the customer
- shows value added to the customer
- is unique to the organization

The mission statement defines for its technical workforce the context in which they are working, providing them with a sense of purpose. A Strategic Plan with an effective mission statement provides partners and constituents a sense of the organization's overall purpose, potentially inspiring their interest in supporting the organization.

Strategic Goals

Strategic goals are the first line of implementation toward the organization's mission and vision. They define courses of action and/or end-states that, if accomplished or achieved, will enable the organization to better support its mission and advance toward its vision. Strategic goals should imply some form of change (e.g., improve, enhance, increase, etc.). By definition, strategic goals are broad in scope and deal with high-level issues relevant to the organization's success.

Strategic Objectives

Strategic objectives are an elaboration of a strategic goal, providing a breakdown of the components for accomplishing the goal. Each strategic objective needs to be measurable and provide greater specificity of the strategic goal that the organization is working to achieve. It is also important that strategic objectives reflect the timeframe for their completion, so they are timebound.

Strategic Initiatives

The organizational strategy for achieving goals and objectives is commonly referred to as strategic initiatives. Strategic initiatives can be thought of as the programs, projects, activities, actions, or tasks that the organization undertakes to meet the goals and achieve objectives. The strategic initiatives are the implementation component of the organization's "how," i.e., how it will achieve the objectives needed to fulfill the goals.

Here's a simple example. Let us suppose one has a personal goal to "lead a healthy lifestyle" and one of your objectives might be to "lose 20 pounds in one year." In that objective, the performance measure is weight (pounds) and the target amount is 20 with a target date of 12 months from the start date.

What are the activities, actions, or tasks one could do to ensure the objective? What are the activities that would result in losing weight? Such activities as increasing exercise, decreasing fats in the diet, reducing calories, etc., are part of a strategy for losing weight. They are the strategic initiatives.

In formulating strategic initiatives, consider these questions:

- Do the initiatives logically link day-to-day operations to the agency's goals and objectives? Do they chart a course to get the agency from today to its delivering results?
- Do they describe what resources (e.g., human, capital, information, funding) are required to achieve the goals and objectives?
- Do they describe whether programs or activities need to be created, eliminated, or restructured to achieve goals and objectives?

Organizations rely on initiatives to achieve their objectives and reach their goals. In fact, many federal-sector agencies begin their strategic planning/performance management efforts with initiative development - a bad idea. Mission and strategic goals should always come first. Next up are strategic objectives and performance measures which tell us what to excel at in order to meet the objective. Targets supply our aims for tracking progress. Strategy/initiatives are put in place to help us achieve the objective. Fulfilling the objective means we will meet the goal and achieve the mission.

Key Performance Indicators

Key performance indicators should be included in the Strategic Plan for tracking the organization's progress. When reviewed on a routine basis, these indicators can help identify potential problem areas in advance so that corrective action is taken before impacting the program. This review demonstrates to stakeholders that the organization is committed to responsibly managing its resources, enhancing its credibility. Government organizations have a responsibility for being transparent and accountable to the public as they spend taxpayer's money. Openly tracking the performance measures established in the Strategic Plan can help provide the necessary transparency and accountability.

KEY CONCEPT: Key performance indicators should be used to measure an important aspect or commodity that represents the achievement of a strategic goal.

Key performance indicators should be designed to measure an important aspect or commodity that represents the type of progress being made toward achieving the strategic goal. These indicators should be related to, but not duplicate all of the detail in project performance measures. In accordance with Principle #3 for realizing where less can be more, too many performance measures at the organization level can become hard to comprehend and difficult to integrate into a collective understanding. There is potentially more clarity possible with fewer performance indicators to help senior leadership and management integrate across the individual programs and functions to obtain a more strategic perspective of the organization. The more detailed project performance measures should be covered in the corresponding implementation plans. Constructing these key performance indicators will be discussed further in Chapter 4.

An organization should first determine "what" it is trying to achieve. The "what" is defined in its vision, mission statement, and strategic goals. These provide the focus for the organization's workforce and their efforts. Meanwhile, strategic objectives and initiatives, i.e., strategies, describe "how" the organization will achieve the "what." It is important that the organization first defines what it is interested in achieving to ensure that the strategies it develops have the appropriate context. Developing strategies without the guidance provided by a vision, mission statement, and goals are likely to be suboptimal and result in wasted resources. Be sure that the organization's "what" is well defined and communicated to ensure the effective design and implementation of the "how."

KEY CONCEPT: Vision statements, mission statements, and strategic goals answer the "what" questions, i.e., what does the organization want to achieve? Strategic objectives and initiatives answer the "how" questions, i.e., how will the organization do it? DO NOT CONFUSE DEFINING THE "WHAT" VS. THE "HOW."

Combined top-down/bottom-up strategic planning

We recommend using a combined top-down/bottom-up approach when creating a Strategic Plan. Senior leadership and management provide the top-down portion in terms of vision, mission, and goals, while the technical workforce provides the bottom-up portion in terms of strategic objectives, initiatives and corresponding performance measures (see Figure 3).

**SENIOR LEADERSHIP &
MANAGEMENT'S VISION**

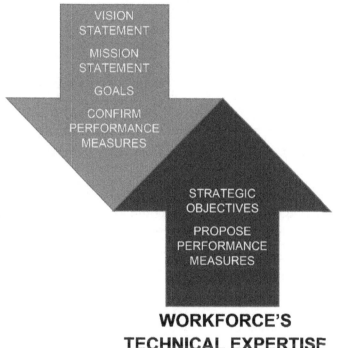

**WORKFORCE'S
TECHNICAL EXPERTISE
OPERATIONAL KNOWLEDGE**

Figure 3. Effective strategic planning involves a combined Top-Down / Bottom-Up approach.

The role for senior leadership and management is to define the vision, mission, and goals that describe the organization's purpose. This is senior leadership and management's opportunity to communicate to the technical workforce, stakeholders, constituents, and partners what they believe the organization should accomplish. Senior leadership and management may express their priorities verbally to staff, stakeholders, and constituents, but the Strategic Plan provides a clear and concise record of their expectations for all to see, examine, and provide feedback. This is the top-down contribution to the strategic planning process.

KEY CONCEPT: Senior leadership and management provide the top-down portion in terms of vision, mission, and goals, while the technical workforce provides the bottom-up portion in terms of strategic objectives, initiatives, and corresponding performance measures.

Managers within the technical workforce are then asked to provide their assessment of the feasibility for achieving the proposed mission and goals, based on their past experience and expertise. This is the bottom-up contribution to the strategic planning process. The technical workforce help determine whether the organization has adequate capability, facilities, workforce, and other needed resources to accomplish the mission and goals. This provides valuable input to leadership in refining or adjusting the mission and goals, or determining what technical or resource gaps need to be filled. For added background on top-down versus bottom-up see Sabatier (1986) and Long and Franklin (2004).

Having clear goals is important to achieving success. What better way for leadership to determine if the organization's goals are clear than to receive feedback from its technical workforce on the goals it defined during the strategic planning process? Along with helping to technically calibrate the leadership's mission and goals, considering the technical workforce's suggestions increases their sense of ownership in the organization vision, mission, and goals. This involvement of the technical workforce can be very motivational in working with senior leadership and management toward the organization's success. Involving the technical workforce in helping refine the mission statement and goals is consistent with Principle #1.

APPLICATION OF PRINCIPLE #1 (INVOLVEMENT): Involving the technical workforce in refining the mission statement and goals can help increase their ownership of the mission and goals, and motivation to fulfill the vision.

Employing a Strategic Plan Framework

To facilitate this exchange of ideas in the strategic planning process, develop a Strategic Plan Framework that outlines the mission, goals, and strategic objectives necessary for realizing the organization's vision (see Figure 4).

Figure 4. An example of the main components of a strategic plan framework

Senior leadership and management can use the Strategic Plan Framework to identify their top-down priorities by providing the proposed mission and goals. They can create their own goals or mark up the framework from the prior Strategic Plan. The Strategic Plan Framework can be shared among the technical workforce electronically, posted online for video or teleconferenced discussions.

Involving the technical workforce in aligning their capabilities to the achievement of the related goals in the framework helps them see where their contribution fits in securing the success of the organization. As the technical workforce provide the implementation skills, abilities, and efforts, they are in the best position to add the corresponding strategic objectives as the stepping stones for accomplishing the goals. In this way, the organization's technical workforce provide a validation of the mission and goals presented in the Strategic Plan Framework by considering whether or not the organization has the means for achieving those goals. Per Principle #1, this involvement can help improve their ownership of the goals and motivation to achieve what they have contributed to defining.

APPLICATION OF PRINCIPLE #1 (INVOLVEMENT): Involving the technical workforce in aligning their capabilities to the achievement of the related goals in the framework helps them see where their contribution fits in securing the success of the organization...This can help improve their ownership of the goals and motivation to achieve what they have contributed to defining.

Strategic Plan Frameworks are also valuable tools for consulting with external stakeholders, constituents, and partners. Attempting to have a large external audience review and comment on a fully developed strategic plan document can be daunting, potentially generating a myriad of very specific comments that would not be reflected at the strategic level. These comments may also be arriving late in the process after many internal agreements and decisions have already been made. Employing a Strategic Plan Framework for consultation with stakeholders, constituents, and partners, provides an opportunity for external parties to identify their issues upfront at the start of the planning process. In this way, external input can be considered as part of the plan's development, and included in the drafts that are reviewed for approval by the organization's executives, managers, and workforce.

Review: Steps for creating a Strategic Plan

- Start by having your planning and performance team draft an outline for the organization in terms of mission, goals, and strategic objectives in a Strategic Plan Framework based on the organization's senior leadership and management's vision (defining goals and strategic objectives will be discussed further in the next chapter).
- Review the Strategic Plan Framework among members of senior leadership and management to help shape the top-down portion of the Strategic Plan.
- Share the Strategic Plan Framework with the technical workforce for their comments to help further refine and validate the goals. These collaborative discussions provide opportunities to develop further understanding among the participants of the mission and goals, and a chance for senior leadership and management to hear from the technical workforce on what capabilities are available vs. what more might be needed.
- Request key performance indicators from the corresponding technical managers and/or directors. Be sure to organize these hierarchically, so that the more detailed measures tracked within each program provide input to the more broadly scoped key performance indicators. Remember it is important that all the key performance indicators are meaningful to the decision makers and technical workforce in their assessment of progress toward achieving success.
- Review final draft of the Strategic Plan with senior leadership and management, and any necessary stakeholders.

In accordance with Principle #3 for recognizing where less can be more, the appropriate level of detail should be matched with the corresponding level of management. The same principle should be applied to producing the Strategic Plan. The Strategic Plan should provide an overarching, organization-wide perspective, comparable to that of senior leadership and management. There can be a tendency to include too many details in the Strategic Plan. If there are too many details, the clarity needed to recognize the organization's overarching strategic perspective of its mission, goals, strategic objectives, and corresponding performance measures can be lost.

There can be a temptation to insert tactical details into the Strategic Plan. Resist this temptation! Tactical details are more appropriate for program and project implementation plans. Functions such as human capital, information technology, financial management, acquisition, and administrative support are means to an end (i.e., tactical), and are more meaningful when discussed within the context of how they affect results of a program or project.

The Strategic Plan provides an opportunity to convey a holistic perspective on what all of the organization's components are working together to achieve, so as to help unify the components' technical contributors toward a common overarching purpose. This is the role for leadership and management we believe was envisioned by organization theorists Henri Fayol (1916), Luther Gulick (1937), and Herbert Simon (1976) to benefit from the division of labor among technical specialists. Such a holistic perspective helps individuals across the agency see where they contribute to the achievement of the organization. There is also a benefit to conveying a clear and concise description to stakeholders and constituents of what goals the organization is trying to achieve and an outline of how to get there. The plan to achieve these goals is substantiated by a commitment to track and report interim progress using key performance indicators identified in the Strategic Plan.

Key points

- A Strategic Plan can help senior leadership and management translate their vision for the organization into more operational terms of mission and goals.

- The Strategic Plan Framework can be used to engage the technical workforce in helping refine the mission and goals, and provide strategic objectives that define the means for achieving the goals.

- A combined top-down/bottom-up approach applies the knowledge of the technical workforce in refining the senior leadership and management's vision. This helps align the organization's technical capabilities with the visionary goals, better ensuring success while promoting ownership of the goals throughout the organization.

- Apply the appropriate level of detail to the corresponding level of management in the organization. This helps to best utilize the different skills and organizational perspectives across the organization.

- It is important that a Strategic Plan provides the holistic vision and overall roadmap for the organization, and is not confused by too many tactical details which can be more effectively provided in supplemental specialized documents.

- Strategic Plan Frameworks provide a template for helping communicate online and facilitating discussion via video or teleconferencing as necessary. This is especially helpful for geographically dispersed organizations.

Chapter 3: Determining Strategic Goals and Strategic Objectives

Determining Strategic Goals

Strategic goals encapsulate the benefits the organization will provide to the public through its activities. Producing these benefits to the public forms the purpose for the organization's existence. Goals, developed as part of the Strategic Plan Framework, reflect the changing level of a condition or commodity (e.g., crime, injury, health, homelessness, etc.) as an outcome of the organization's actions. Therefore, these goals are referred to as outcome-oriented.

The Center for American Progress' (www.americanprogress.org) "Doing What Works" initiative demonstrated that clearly defined goals are important to achieving success (Kohli, 2010). With clearly defined goals, members of the organization understand the leadership's expectations and the purpose to which they should be applying their skills and efforts. A clearly defined goal increases the probability that everyone in the organization's senior leadership, management, and technical workforce are working toward the same result, as they use the goal to determine which of their activities are relevant to helping the organization be successful. The goal should be clear in its description of what is to be achieved, along with the corresponding quantity, quality, and timeframe.

A good strategic goal:

- covers the agency's major functions and operations, and are consistent with its statutory authorities;
- is results-oriented (e.g., reducing workplace accidents) rather than output or process oriented (e.g., inspecting more workplaces);
- is measurable, i.e., quantitative or otherwise expressed in a way that will permit assessment of whether the goal has been achieved;
- is logically related to the agency's mission; and

- is realistic, i.e., they are within the agency's span of influence and resources.

Common attributes of a good strategic goal statement include the following:

- expressed to facilitate future assessment as to whether the goal was or is being achieved
- is open-ended
- is outcome or results oriented

In writing strategic goals, a suggestion is to begin with the word "to" followed by an action verb, such as:

- To develop_____
- To provide_____
- To ensure_____
- To deliver_____

This introduces the desired commodity or benefit to be produced. Here is an example from the NASA 2018 Strategic Plan. These four strategic goals align to four major strategic themes—Discover, Explore, Develop, and Enable—that will achieve NASA's Vision and Mission. They were deliberately chosen to highlight a new era of space exploration and show America's preeminence in space, exploration, science, technology, and aeronautics.

- Discover: [To] Expand human knowledge through new scientific discoveries.
- Explore: [To] Extend human presence deeper into space and to the Moon for sustainable long-term exploration and utilization.
- Develop: [To] Address national challenges and catalyze economic growth.
- Enable: [To] Optimize capabilities and operations.

While each of these strategic goals does not actually start with the word "to", the word is implied and followed by an action verb such as "expand," "extend," "address," and "optimize."

It is important to distinguish programmatic goals from institutional and/or administrative goals. Programmatic goals are those that reflect the accomplishment of the organization's results and benefits (e.g., reduced homelessness, improved water quality, health, welfare, etc.). Institutional and/or administrative goals are more tactical than strategic, providing the means by which the programmatic goals are achieved. Administrative processes for acquisition, financial accounting, budgeting, and human capital management, etc., are captured in tactical goals as important enablers, i.e., means to the ends. These should not be tracked as a substitute for tracking programmatic results. Progress toward tactical institutional and/or administrative goals should be tracked separately to ensure that the programmatic goals receive the appropriate level of attention with stakeholders and constituents. Programmatic goals are more relevant to the organization's senior leadership and management's focus on realizing the vision.

Creating a logic model, as outlined in Figure 5, aligns the organization's means with its ends. This alignment helps confirm that the organization has the appropriate capabilities for producing its outcomes, i.e., achieving its goals, which are reflected on the right side of the logic model.

Figure 5. Logic models can be used to determine if the organization has adequate abilities to achieve its outcomes/goals.

The logic model begins on the far-left side of Figure 5 with the resources used by the organization to conduct the processes that will produce the outputs needed for goal achievement. Resources can include funding, amount of labor, levels and types of expertise, time, as well as stakeholder guidance and operating authorities. Shortages of resources (i.e., the inputs) for conducting the necessary processes need to be identified so that additional resources can be acquired or the corresponding outcome adjusted to what is available.

Moving one step to the right in Figure 5 are the organization's processes that produce outputs. Processes can include such activities as planning and design, development or production, deployment and operations, review and testing, etc. For the military, these processes can include the development and/or acquisition of weapons, training of soldiers, transportation or deployment, all of which are means to the ends of protecting the country.

Next, to the right of the processes in Figure 5 is the list of outputs. These outputs reflect what the technical workforce are producing and/or delivering through their processes. The production of these outputs leads to realization of the outcomes and the organization's goals. In these outputs, the technical workforce begin to see how their efforts affect the achievement of the outcomes, the organization's goals.

It is important to distinguish outputs relative to outcomes. For example, outputs can take the form of a grant being issued, service being delivered, a highway or bridge being built, report being published, regulation being established, etc. Some examples are provided in Table 1.

Table 1. Examples of outputs vs. outcomes

OUTPUTS	OUTCOMES
Permits issued	Increased recreation Resources mined
Grant funding distributed	Reduced homelessness Reduced individuals without food Reduced cases of illness (via research discoveries)
Job training sessions completed	Increased employment

While outcome-based goals are preferred in the Strategic Plan, they can be challenging to define in quantifiable terms for some government programs. For example, a program can have a goal of improving the quality of life, increasing knowledge, reducing the negative impact of poverty, improving health, providing a safe and secure homeland, or reducing the occurrence of destructive acts. But how much of an increase or decrease is considered effective, and can it be definitively measured? In these cases, consider the quantifiable aspect of the program that is closest to representing the achievement of the goal, especially if it is managerially meaningful. "Managerially meaningful" refers to decisions that are under the direct control or influence of the workforce that affect the amount of production or service provided. While the level of poverty is the desired outcome, measuring the number of homeless individuals who are provided shelter, or number of individuals fed by assistance programs may be more managerially meaningful and more practical to measure. The degree of safety experienced by the members of a community may be difficult to quantify, while a reduction in crime incidents may be more measurable and an informative substitute to use for the goal.

The logic model provides a tool for assessing whether the organization has the means for producing and/or delivering the outputs needed to achieve the outcomes. If there are outputs for which there is not a corresponding process that can adequately produce the output, then adjustments are needed either to the goal or to the organization's capabilities. This planning step helps in better ensuring the organization has the practical means to be successful. For more information on logic models, see W.K. Kellogg Foundation (2004).

Determining Strategic Objectives

The technical workforce can use their outputs to help define the strategic objectives in the Strategic Plan Framework. These strategic objectives reflect the practical steps for achieving the goals. This demonstrates that the organization has devised a method for achieving its goals and accomplishing its mission which is documented for all to see in the Strategic Plan. Stakeholders, partners, and constituents recognize that with these practical steps defined, the organization has a more realistic probability of success and is worthy of their support.

Common attributes of a good strategic objective statement include the following:

- expressed in a way to facilitate future assessment as to whether the goal was or is being achieved
- close-ended (contains an achievement date)
- directly measurable

Although strategic objectives are written in many ways, it is critical that strategic objectives should have four distinct, easily-identifiable parts:

- direction of change
- performance measure/metric
- target value
- target date

Strategic objectives should start out with a single word that indicates a direction of change. In its simplest format, that means words like "increase" or "decrease," or variations such as "expand" or "reduce." An ideal strategic objective should also include a performance measure/metric with a target value and a target date.

For example, consider the following typical strategic objective for an agency's Chief Information Officer or Information Technology (IT) Helpdesk:

> "Decrease IT Helpdesk Customer Call Waiting Time to 45 seconds or less by FY 2022."

The four distinct parts of that strategic objectives should be easily-identifiable.

- Direction of change: Decrease
- Performance measure/metric: IT Helpdesk Customer Call Waiting Time
- Target amount: 45 Seconds or less
- Target date: FY 2022

Strategic objectives written in this manner are clear statements of what senior leadership wants to achieve in order to accomplish a strategic goal. Progress toward achieving these strategic objectives will be tracked with performance measures. As such, strategic objectives help define the performance measures, to be discussed further in Chapter 4.

Key points

- Defining clear goals is essential to the success of the organization.
- Goals should be based on the senior leadership and management's vision for what the organization should achieve.
- Clear goals communicate the purpose of the organization to members of the organization, stakeholders, and constituents, and can help guide the technical workforce in conducting their efforts, facilitate coordination, and promote support for the organization.
- Distinguish programmatic goals from institutional and administrative goals to ensure that the appropriate level of focus is maintained on the organization's end outcome results/benefits and the main purpose for its existence.
- Employing a logic model can help confirm the organization has the capabilities for realizing the goals (outcomes) defined by senior leadership and management.
- Outputs reflect the products from the technical workforce's use of resources in conducting processes. These outputs can be used to define the strategic objectives as stepping stones to achieving the goals defined in the Strategic Plan.
- Involving the technical workforce in determining the strategic objectives provides another opportunity to insert their expertise in ensuring the technical feasibility of the Strategic Plan. This technical validation improves the probabilities for success, improves the technical workforce's ownership and motivation for achieving the organization's goals, and promotes support from stakeholders, partners, and constituents.
- Quantifying outcome goals can be challenging. In these cases, measuring a managerially meaningful output may be needed as a representative indicator of the outcome.

Chapter 4: Designing Performance Measures

Once strategic goals and strategic objectives have been created for the Strategic Plan Framework and the organization's capabilities verified in the logic model, it is important to track progress using performance measures. The performance measures used to track the amounts of the outputs produced and outcomes achieved should be included in the Strategic Plan. These performance measures help the organization's senior leadership, management, and technical workforce effectively manage their activities. Performance measures provide a relatively more objective basis from which conversations can be conducted on "how are we doing," "are we on-track," and whether success has been achieved. Information in the performance measures provides the proof of what would otherwise be a more subjective personal opinion, i.e., "I think we are doing well." These discussions on progress and goal achievement among senior leadership, management, and the technical workforce enable a more active form of management assisting coordination, collaboration, and engagement across the multiple levels of the organization. This interaction can help better ensure success in realizing the vision for the organization.

Tracking interim progress on a routine basis can help identify potential problems before achieving the goal is threatened. This allows for preemptive mid-course adjustments to help better ensure success. In monitoring its progress and taking corresponding action where needed, the organization demonstrates to its stakeholders, constituents, and partners that it is a responsible steward of the resources being provided, is committed to achieving its mission in the most effective manner possible, and worthy of their support.

Performance measures should be developed using the following five design characteristics:

- Able to reliably count the quantity of a commodity or effect produced due to the organization's actions;
- Recognized as meaningful/useful by leadership, workforce, stakeholders, and constituents;

- Applied/tracked routinely in practice;
- Measurable at a reasonable cost; and
- Possess a verifiable approach of measurement.

Each of these design characteristics are described in the following sections.

Design Characteristic #1: Able to reliably count a commodity or effect produced due to the organization's actions

Performance measures should track the amount of a commodity or effect produced in achieving an objective or goal. These objectives and goals were identified in the Strategic Plan Framework in support of accomplishing the mission. In this way, the organization has the means for regularly tracking its progress and determining whether alternate actions are needed to better ensure that the mission is accomplished and the vision realized.

The primary types of performance measures include:

- Quantity – a count of the amount of a commodity or attribute;
- Quality – a count of the degree to which a commodity or attribute meets a specified standard, or the count of a commodity or attribute that meets a specified standard;
- Efficiency – the amount of a commodity or attribute that has been produced, achieved, acquired, or produced per a period of time, dollar amount, or other criteria; and
- Timebound – the amount of time taken to produce or acquire a specified amount of a commodity or attribute, or percent accomplished within a timeframe; i.e., timeliness.

An example of each performance measure type is provided in Table 2.

Table 2. Examples primary types of performance measures

TYPE OF PERFORMANCE MEASURE	EXAMPLE
Quantity	Percent of acres restored to specified condition
Quality	Percent of acres restored to "high" (i.e., greater than specified) condition
Efficiency	Percent of acres restored within a range of $___ to $___ per acre
Timebound	Percent of acres restored within a specified time period

In designing performance measures, it is important to specify the criteria by which a commodity or attribute can be counted as being successfully produced, achieved, or acquired. This includes specifying what constitutes an improvement and how much of an improvement is needed to be counted by the measure as successful. For example, in attempting to improve public health, the change in the amount of the population afflicted with a certain condition or disease could be measured. Present levels can be compared against a rolling average of the past 3-5 years. A threshold of what is considered a successful achievement would be defined by senior leadership management in the Strategic Plan, such as a 1% reduction, or 5%, reduction, etc.

Be sure to consider the extent to which the measured result is due to the actions of the organization. There are often contributing factors, external to the organization and beyond its control, that can also affect the result. Care must be taken to control for or at least define the effect of such related factors so as to not confound the results. Some examples of other contributing factors affecting results include:

- environmental (e.g., temperature, humidity, air quality, etc.)
- economical (e.g., how much of the target population can afford adequate food, shelter, or treatments)
- social (e.g., how much of the target population has a predisposition to the condition due to family history, possesses medical insurance, or is willing to accept treatment, etc.)
- changes to the size of the population

There is frequently an interest in using efficiency measures especially in counting the quantity of outputs or outcomes achieved per increment of time or funding. Such efficiency measures may be used to try and determine if an adequate value is being realized. The cost-per-unit of performance might be compared across multiple programs to try to determine which program is "better managed." However, many government programs might not be readily comparable on a cost-per-unit basis, especially for those with cases of varying complexities requiring widely differing levels of effort and/or resources. For example, agencies protecting against wildland fire have found that more remote areas can be treated at a lower cost-per-acre than areas closer to populated areas. The areas that are closer to populated areas require a more meticulous and thorough manual approach which is more expensive than that used in more remote areas. The risk tolerance is lower when treating populated areas vs. the more remote areas, resulting in a very justifiable and reasonable difference in treatment costs-per-acre.

In developing viable performance measures for tracking the organization's progress, be aware that achieving outcomes could require multiple years of effort, while the outputs may be produced on a more annual timeframe. For example, reforesting an area after a fire or other destructive natural event (i.e., the output) may take at least one or two growing seasons to determine if the effort was successful (i.e., the outcome). This is especially relevant when developing performance measures for supporting the annual budget process. Even when government agency strategic and budget plans include a five-year horizon, legislatures may only appropriate funds for a one or two-year increment.

While the outcome-oriented performance measures may consider more long-term results, output-oriented performance measures may be more helpful in tracking nearer term progress closer to the timing of the appropriation approval cycle. Without the addition of output measures, where multiple years are needed to achieve the outcome results, there could be a long time during which performance is not measured while waiting for the goal's multiple-year finish line. Such near-term performance measures can help identify the potential need for mid-course programmatic or resource adjustments, or help inform budget estimates where the goal covers multiple annual budget cycles. Therefore, be sure to develop performance measures to cover both output production and end outcome achievement. For either type of measure, there should be a recognizable linkage between the commodity or condition being measured and goal achievement.

However, while both output and outcome performance measures are needed, sometimes organizations focus too much on measuring the conduct of their activities than the quantity of results they produce. This can be prevalent in grant issuing government organizations, where the organization may focus its performance measures more on the process for attaining the funds, reviewing applications, and issuing the grants than the level of results produced after the grant is applied. Be sure to not only measure the level of successful process activities, but the quantity of the benefits being achieved with the funds provided by the organization's grants. Examples of both output and outcome performance measures are provided in Table 3.

Table 3. Examples of output vs. outcome performance measures

OUTPUT (PROCESS) MEASURES	OUTCOME (GOAL/RESULTS) MEASURES
Housing units surveyed Plans completed/units ready to be restored Units restored	Homelessness (percent of individuals)

Design Characteristic #2: Recognized as meaningful/useful by leadership, workforce, stakeholders, and constituents

To be effective, performance measures need to be recognized as meaningful/useful by:

- senior leadership and management for insight into the progress being made by the multiple programs they oversee;
- technical workforce interested in seeing and communicating what progress is being made within their unit and related units with which they collaborate; and
- stakeholders and constituents in helping them determine whether to support the organization and its programs.

The best sources of performance measures are the individuals whose own performance will be judged by the measure, and used in their decision-making. The technical workforce need to agree that the performance measures accurately reflect the results of their work (also see Solan, 2009). If they do not find the performance measures meaningful, they will not support them and the organization's use of performance measures fails. If the measurements are useful to the technical workforce, they will support the measurements for their own purposes as well as the organization's purposes. Just as involving the technical workforce in developing the Strategic Plan Framework and the organization's goals is important, their involvement in selecting the performance measures is also important. Their involvement better ensures the measures are useful in tracking the organization's progress and increases their engagement in pursuing the organization's goals (Principle #1). While the technical workforce should propose the performance measures to use, senior leadership and management should determine if the proposed performance measures meet their expectations for determining whether the organization's goals are being achieved (also see Lu, 2008). Now, the technical workforce, senior leadership, and management are all collaborating on how to best ensure achieving the organization's goals in accordance with Principle #2 for active management.

APPLICATION OF PRINCIPLES #1 (INVOLVEMENT) and #2 (ACTIVE MANAGEMENT): While the technical workforce should propose the performance measures to use, senior leadership and management should determine if the proposed performance measures meet their expectations for determining whether the organization's goals are being achieved.

APPLICATION OF PRINCIPLE #3 (LESS CAN BE MORE): For senior leadership and management, key performance indicators may be more useful to their organization-wide perspective, and further their use of performance information.

For senior leadership and management, key performance indicators may be more useful to their organization-wide perspective. Rather than trying to navigate the full range of details across the organization's various programs, this subset of performance indicators can help engage senior leadership and management in determining where their attention is most needed. Presenting senior leadership and management with too much performance information, especially without an organized construct, can deter their interest in using performance information. Without leadership interest in using performance information, the rest of the organization can lose interest in maintaining and using performance information at the potential detriment to the organization's success. In this case, less can be more when engaging senior leadership and management in the effective use of performance measures (per Principle #3).

Figure 6. Contributors to a key performance indicator on managing land condition.

For illustration purposes, consider a key performance indicator for lands being managed by a government agency such as the Department of the Interior, depicted in Figure 6. The public lands across the bureaus may have different priorities and types, e.g., uplands, wetlands, surface water, desert lands, etc., across numerous locations where tailored definitions of desired condition are documented in local land management plans. While the condition for any specific collection of acres is of particular interest and the responsibility of the local manager, a collective measurement of the total acreage in desired condition across all managed areas could be adequate for most strategic discussions at the Department level. An executive decision maker could employ a key performance indicator of "acres in desired condition" to attain an overall perspective to help determine where he/she needs to explore further. The more detailed supporting data would be available for further analysis as particular issues were identified.

Along with key performance indicators, a more strategic organization-wide perspective may be provided by creating an index. An index provides a single representative value that combines several factors, commodities, attributes, and/or conditions in a ratio. The user has one numerical figure to assess rather than trying to interpret the relative contributions of several individual factors. Familiar examples include the Consumer Price Index based on the average price of a basket of consumer goods, or the Gross Domestic Product which combines the effects of personal consumption, business investments, government spending, and net exports. Another example, the Facility Condition Index is frequently used to convey the worthiness of repairing vs. replacing a building or structure. The Facility Condition Index provides a ratio of the estimated cost of needed repairs relative to the cost of reconstructing the building or structure. The closer the ratio is to 1.0, the more reconstructing the building or structure is justified as opposed to implementing the various repairs.

Design Characteristic #3: Applied/tracked routinely in practice

Performance measures are the tools by which members of senior leadership, management, and the technical workforce are able to objectively determine progress toward the goals in the Strategic Plan, and discuss what action may be needed to better ensure success. These discussions provide opportunities for collaboration and coordination, and need to occur on a regularly reoccurring basis as part of the organization's active management practices. Such discussions need to be promoted by senior leadership and management through their participation, so that the technical workforce recognize performance measurement as an important part of routine operations and practice.

Targets will be needed to help benchmark whether adequate progress is being made toward producing the output, or achieving the outcome in accordance with the organization's mission as defined in the Strategic Plan. These targets should be based on the level of progress expected for each period (i.e., quarterly, monthly, annually) in order to achieve the strategic objective. Annual performance measure targets should be developed at the start of the program to be updated each year as part of the annual budget formulation process. Quarterly or monthly performance measure targets should be developed at the start of each fiscal year to correspond with the annual budget as proposed or appropriated.

Some targets reflect an estimated level of performance expected to be achieved, as a projection of what could be accomplished. Other targets may be used as a reference point for assessing progress, while not necessarily attempting to predict the level of accomplishment. These targets may use past actual experience as a benchmark for comparisons of performance. For example, targets for public injury rates may reflect achieving a level that is less than the average injury rate for the past three years. This type of target is useful where predicting a quantifiable level of achievement is too challenging (e.g., death or injury rates, computer security intrusions, crime rates, etc.).

The organization's technical workforce should propose the targets that will be used for measuring their programs' or functions' progress during a specified timeframe. Senior leadership and management should review these targets for consistency with their expectations for achieving the goals established in the Strategic Plan and accomplishing the mission. This ties the technical workforce directly into determining whether the senior leadership and management's goals can be accomplished. Comparing actual measured progress against these targets can help determine potential issues in advance so that alternate actions can be planned and executed before a more damaging problem occurs. Tracking the progress relative to a target, or estimated level of performance, provides a tangible objective basis for discussion rather than subjective opinions.

Design Characteristic #4: Measurable at a reasonable cost

Performance measurements may be made directly or conducted through parametric methods including sampling. For example, it may be cost prohibitive to measure the condition of every square inch of the lake and stream surfaces in a state or nationally. However, taking a sampling of measurements from a collection of sensors in a lake or stream can be used as a representative indicator of the overall condition. This is based on having the appropriate scientific research and justification for extrapolating the results from the samples to a larger total area. Similarly, rather than bearing the cost of trying to survey the entire population's opinion on a topic, polls may target a statistically representative sample of the population.

Another potential cost driver is the means for collecting and managing performance data. Data collection can become more complex and costly depending upon the geographic area over which the organization operates (e.g., the Department of the Interior manages 20% of the Unites States with 2,400 locations across the country). Automated performance data collection systems should accurately collect, accumulate, store, and transmit data as operations are conducted, rather than as a separate after-the-fact data call/request. However, the performance data being collected needs to be considered useful by the workforce to promote their participation, while also being informative to senior leadership and management.

Design Characteristic #5: Possess a verifiable approach of measurement

With any performance management process, it is necessary to demonstrate the validity of the performance measures and data. This validation ensures confidence that the performance information accurately counts the commodities produced, represents the organization's efforts, and is reliable for management decision-making. The corresponding credibility is a key attribute necessary for an organization to obtain support for its programs.

Documenting the performance measures' definition of terms and methods of measurement helps to demonstrate the organization's commitment to ensuring the validity of its assessments. Stakeholders and constituents need to recognize these measurements are reliable in providing information for decision-making and finding potential problems in advance to better ensure the organization's success. Descriptive information provided for each performance measure should minimally include:

- description of what is being measured
- description of the measure's relationship to producing an output or outcome and achieving a goal
- definition of any technical terms used in the measure
- source of the data for the measure (include any measurement device that may be used, and who or what organizational units collect the data)
- frequency for collecting data

- description of sampling, estimation, or parametric modeling methods that are routinely applied, specifying which variables are actual, and which are estimated/extrapolated
- validation history/experience (over the last three years)

Documenting the processes for confirming the validity of the data is also important. Such techniques include:

- identifying and analyzing observations of unexpected or sizeable difference in trends from one year to another;
- in-depth reviews of factors behind largely different cases, especially across collections of cases expected to be more similar;
- site visits to confirm that the reported data is consistent with conditions experienced at the site; and
- investigating a sampling of cases to confirm validity of data sources and data collection methods.

Creating an office of analysts who understand the organization's programmatic activities could help conduct such assessments across the organization while minimizing the distraction to the workforce conducting the programs.

Key points

- Performance measures are needed to track the organization's progress toward reaching its objectives and achieving its goals.
- Performance measures should be developed for the outputs and the outcomes that are defined in the logic model, reflecting the results of actions taken by the organization.
- Important characteristics of effective performance measures include:
  - o able to reliably count the quantity of a commodity or effect produced due to the organization's actions;
  - o recognized as meaningful/useful by leadership, workforce, stakeholders, and constituents;

- o applied/tracked routinely in practice;
- o measurable at a reasonable cost; and
- o possess a verifiable approach of measurement.
- Performance measures and the corresponding targets are best developed by the technical workforce who implement the programs being tracked, as long as the performance measures are confirmed to be useful by senior leadership and management for decision-making.
- Senior leadership and management need to be involved in endorsing targets and routine reviews of progress using the performance measures to help determine whether adequate progress is being made toward achieving the goals and accomplishing the mission defined in the Strategic Plan.

Chapter 5: Performance Assessment Techniques

We need to apply the performance measures and their targets to determine the amount of progress and whether it is adequate for successfully achieving the objectives. The following performance assessment techniques can be used to apply the data provided by performance measures into information for decision-making. This chapter will describe each technique, its application, and the perspectives to be gained. The performance assessment techniques to be discussed are:

- Routine plan vs. actual tracking
- Red/Yellow/Green assessment
- Comparing performance and funding trends over multiple years

Routine plan vs. actual tracking

One approach for assessing the progress of an activity is by comparing the actual rates of monthly or quarterly accomplishment with the corresponding expected rates of accomplishment (the plan), using a pair of line graphs. This is referred to as routine plan vs. actual tracking.

The amounts of cumulative progress expected for each month or quarter during the year are graphed on one line. The planned, or expected, amounts of progress are plotted along the vertical Y-axis (ordinate) for each corresponding interval (month or quarter) plotted along the horizontal X-axis (abscissa). A second line plots the actual amount of progress experienced for each time interval. Each data point along the second line will be compared against the corresponding data point on the line that was initially plotted for the expected amount of progress during the same time interval. The distance between the two data points indicates the potential severity of the program's problems. If the actual amount of progress achieved is less than the expected (planned) amount of progress for the time interval, adjustments to workflow, processes, and/or program resources are needed. These adjustments can help make up for the delay in performance and better ensure achieving the desired levels of accomplishment. If appropriate, adjustments to the subsequent monthly or quarterly plans may be needed to provide a more realistic projection of the future timing for achieving program results. However, the need for too many adjustments to the plan should be considered carefully to determine if more serious and substantial changes to the program are needed.

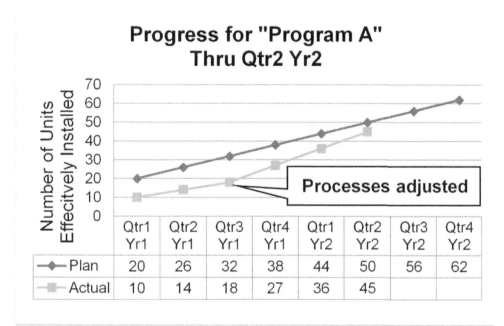

Progress for "Program A" Thru Qtr2 Yr2

	Qtr1 Yr1	Qtr2 Yr1	Qtr3 Yr1	Qtr4 Yr1	Qtr1 Yr2	Qtr2 Yr2	Qtr3 Yr2	Qtr4 Yr2
Plan	20	26	32	38	44	50	56	62
Actual	10	14	18	27	36	45		

Figure 7. Example of routine Plan vs. Actual tracking

The example in Figure 7 displays the quarterly status for Program A. Estimates for the number of units to be installed each quarter, which deliver the benefits of Program "A," are plotted on the line labelled "Plan." The number of units effectively installed through the second quarter of the second year is reflected on the line labelled "Actual." In reviewing the line graphs, senior leadership, management, and the technical workforce noticed that the actual number of units effectively installed (i.e., 18 units) was lagging behind the expected plan (i.e., 32 units) through the first three quarters of the first year (i.e., Qtr1 Yr1 through Qtr3 Yr1). As a result, adjustments were made to the program in Qtr4 Yr1. These adjustments could involve increasing resources (i.e., workforce, funding, etc.) or adjusting the workflow. The rate of units effectively installed increased in subsequent quarters, as reflected by the "actual" line sloping closer to the "plan" line. If this rate of progress continues, by projecting the actual line to continue on its new slope, the program should achieve the original planned level of results expected by the end of the second year.

PRO: This is a straight-forward visual assessment technique that directly applies the performance measures developed as part of the strategic planning and reporting process. The expected level of progress to be achieved each month or quarter would have been provided by the technical workforce and approved by senior leadership and management. Routine plan vs. actual tracking should be consistent with the organization's mission and vision as it is based on the strategic objectives and performance measures established as part of the strategic planning process. The technique can provide advance notice that corrective action is needed prior to the program's completion date. The plan can also be adjusted where the technical workforce and senior leadership and management agree that a more realistic projection of expectations for future progress is needed, based on a better understanding of the program's abilities and/or challenges being faced. In these ways, routine plan vs. actual tracking is a useful tool helping senior leadership, management, and the technical workforce jointly assess interim progress and make adjustments to better ensure that the program is successfully conducted.

CON: This technique's effectiveness depends upon the abilities of senior leadership, senior management, and the technical workforce to define a plan for the future despite uncertainties in resource availability, unexpected technical challenges, and changes in operating conditions. The willingness to estimate future performance can be impeded by concerns of potential criticism for failing to achieve the estimated level of progress despite unforeseen changes in conditions that are not necessarily under the organization's control.

While attempting to develop future estimates of performance can be scary, the emphasis should be more on creating projections that are managerially useful rather than exceedingly accurate. The planned amounts of progress for each time interval are needed to provide some benchmark to judge whether adequate progress is being made and if adjustments are needed to better ensure success. In developing estimates of future performance for assessment purposes, referencing past history can sometimes provide a benchmark for indicating whether performance is increasing, or remaining steady, relative to past experience. Another technique involves dividing an end goal of the program by the number of time intervals during its implementation, e.g., taking the end-of-year goal and dividing by 12 for monthly progress assessments or dividing by 4 for quarterly assessments. This targeting approach provides an indication of whether a steady rate of progress is being achieved, assuming that it is adequate for reaching the desired end-of-year result.

APPLICATION OF PRINCIPLES: Employing routine plan vs. actual tracking to assess interim performance applies all three guiding principles.

PRINCIPLE #1 (INVOLVEMENT): Having technical workforce create and track their plan for potential progress infuses their expert knowledge into reviewing progress toward the specified goals. This improves their ownership and motivation toward achieving the defined goals.

PRINCIPLE #2 (ACTIVE MANAGEMENT): Involving the senior leadership and management with the technical workforce in jointly reviewing progress and determining future action exercises active management.

PRINCIPLE #3 (LESS CAN BE MORE): The graph focuses on a key performance indicator to compare progress against expectations in a clear, straight-forward manner which facilitates understanding and productive discussion.

Red/Yellow/Green assessments

Another assessment technique involves associating the technical manager's judgement of an activity's progress and prospects for success under one of three colors: red, yellow, or green.

Red – indicates the activity is experiencing or expecting significant difficulties that will impact the ability to deliver results on-schedule. A recognizable solution has yet to be determined and assistance from senior management and leadership is needed. This could include changes to schedule, scope, approach, and/or resources.

Yellow – indicates the activity is experiencing or expecting challenges that the manager and/or staff believe it can overcome with workarounds and adjustments to schedule and reallocation of resources.

Green – indicates activities where performance is considered to be on-track with no additional assistance needed.

Charts are constructed with each activity listed under its corresponding color category. These charts are presented by technical managers in a status review attended by senior leadership and management (conducting status reviews will be discussed in the next chapter). Summary points can be included to explain the technical manager's rationale for each activity's color designation. Those activities characterized under "green" are considered to be progressing adequately and not in need of too much additional discussion. This display emphasizes discussing those activities that are most in need of attention, characterized as "red," and possibly "yellow." Senior leadership and management determine whether adequate progress is being made toward completing the mission and achieving the vision they created. If not, their assistance will be needed to ensure that the technical workforce have adequate resources and are planning to take the appropriate steps for successful completion.

The prioritization of activities to be discussed helps ensure the meeting is purposeful and that the participants' time is well spent. Without this, the meeting could run longer than needed and risk not addressing the most necessary topics. This discourages future attendance by senior leadership and management. Senior leadership and management's continued participation is necessary to provide their assistance where needed, and reinforce the importance for the technical workforce to continue monitoring performance. This routine tracking of progress helps to better ensure success.

STATUS OF COMMUNITY SERVICES PROGRAMS (QTR, YR)

Potential Major Impact (RED)	Minor Impact Being Addressed (YELLOW)	On-Track (GREEN)
•Program A •Technical issue •Time needed to develop workaround •Amount of delay in delivery uncertain	•Program D •Workforce shortfall •Increased processing time will delay deliveries 6 weeks	•Program B •Likely completion by October this year •Program C •Deliveries underway

Figure 8. Example of a red/yellow/green assessment chart

Figure 8 provides an example of how a red/yellow/green performance assessment chart would look. The status for four community services programs (A, B, C, and D) are displayed. Programs B and C are listed under "green." The technical manager claims that these programs are on-schedule and progressing well. Unless there is a particular question from the audience, no added discussion is needed on these programs. Program D is listed under "yellow," reporting a shortage of skilled workforce. The manager is estimating a delay in deliveries by six weeks. He/she considers the delay is not significant and could be acceptable rather than implementing more costly solutions of hiring additional workforce or purchasing more equipment to increase capacity. Senior leadership and management could agree with his/her assessment, or otherwise provide added resources depending upon how important they believe it is to maintain the original schedule.

The greatest amount of discussion at the status review will likely be on Program A, which is listed under "red." This program appears to have a technical issue requiring additional investigation to determine what actions are needed and how much additional time could be needed. Senior leadership and management have now been informed of the issue, and may need to provide their assistance in the solution. Their assistance could involve providing added resources in reallocating funding to the program or additional experts to help assess the issue and develop potential solutions.

Some technical managers may be hesitant to notify their senior leadership and management of potential or existing problems, hoping to solve the issue before actually reporting it. However, it is important not to wait too long before reporting potentially significant problems, especially if they threaten the success of the activity. While there is typically a fear of receiving negative reprisals when problems arise, waiting too long to report an issue could result in more significant criticism. No one likes to hear about problems although they can, and do, happen. But if it appears that you delayed reporting a known problem, especially if the problem becomes more serious during the delay in reporting, you could receive added criticism for both the problem and irresponsibly withholding information.

PRO: The red/yellow/green performance assessment technique enables direct collaboration among the technical workforce and senior leadership and management attending the progress status review. This direct collaboration employs active management as per Principle #2. At this review, information is interpreted and conveyed in a condensed, readily understandable format. Rather than present the background data for all the program activities, the focus of discussions is more on deciding what action to take on the most demanding cases. In this way, attendees of the progress status review can cover a wide range of programs in a hierarchically organized manner, with emphasis on those activities most in need of attention and assistance. This is especially valuable for the members of senior leadership and management that attend the progress status review. They have a broad range of responsibilities across the entire organization, so arranging the material to emphasize what is most relevant to their strategic role is a better use of their limited time. This more effective use of their time helps enable their participation in the review process, per Principle #3.

CON: This approach is highly dependent upon the interpretations of the technical workforce, their ability to provide informative and useful assessments, and the receptivity of senior leadership and management. Proud program personnel are often shy to admit any possible weakness, potential failings, or need for assistance until absolutely necessary, i.e., when a problem's impact is being experienced. However, effective identification of potential problems in advance could be included as criteria in individual performance assessments, to help foster participation.

APPLICATION OF PRINCIPLES: Employing the red/yellow/green assessment technique employs Principles #2 and #3.

PRINCIPLE #2 (ACTIVE MANAGEMENT): Managers of the technical workforce present their assessments directly to senior leadership and management, who subsequently determine where they may need to assist in better ensuring success.

PRINCIPLE #3 (LESS CAN BE MORE): Providing the technical workforce's performance assessment involves less time for the senior leadership and management to understand rather than trying to interpret numerous data points. As senior leadership and management are responsible for the entire organization, they do not necessarily have time to dwell on detailed data points that do not need their immediate attention.

Comparing performance and funding trends over multiple years

While funds for government organizations are appropriated for one or two years at a time, many government programs require more than a single year to successfully achieve results. For example, many government land management programs implement treatments in one year that can take several growing seasons to fully produce results. A program may be affected by so many factors beyond the organization's control that multiple years of experience are needed to determine whether its actions have been effective. For example, employment and crime prevention programs can be significantly affected by the differing economic conditions from one year to the next. Therefore, we believe it is more useful to consider the trends in performance achieved and funding invested over multiple years.

In Figure 9, the trends in performance and funding can be divided into the following four main categories, used to prioritize which program areas should receive particular attention for possible changes to funding levels or implementation approaches.

- **Increasing Performance and Decreasing Funding:** Program areas with an increasing trend in performance and decreasing trend in funding would typically not need much added attention by senior leadership and management, as this appears to be a case of achieving more for less. Such cases would usually be considered a desirable outcome, unless contrary to senior leadership and management's expectations.

- **Both Increasing (or Decreasing) Performance and Funding:** Similar trends in performance and funding, either increasing or decreasing, are typically considered reasonable. It is expected that with less funding, less can be accomplished, and with more funding, more should be accomplished. Therefore, program areas demonstrating these trends may not need much additional attention, unless the trend is inconsistent with senior leadership and management's expectations. Program areas demonstrating decreasing performance and funding might deserve additional attention if higher performance is desired.

- **Decreasing Performance and Increasing Funding:** Program areas which demonstrate a decreasing trend in performance while funding is increasing demand added attention to better understand why less performance is being targeted as additional funding is planned. This could help indicate those program areas where alternative actions are needed to better achieve performance. However, there can also be cases where these trends are acceptable, e.g., where the effects of additional funding take several more years of investment to realize results, or more sizable and therefore more costly projects are being taken on which can slow the rate of performance relative to past experience. Whatever the reason, areas with decreasing performance and increasing funding should be further explored to be better understood and potentially acted upon.

The performance trend is based on the measurements of a key performance indicator while the funding trend is based on the budget levels for the program area being monitored. The four categories depicted in Figure 9 display past actual performance and funding levels for five years prior to the present year (PY) from PY-1 through PY-5, and future projected performance and funding levels for the present year and the next year PY+1 which is the year for which the budget is being formulated. As these trends relate past actual results to future projections, these graphs provide an opportunity to benchmark future targets against past experience. Substantial changes from the past experience to future projections should be carefully reviewed to ensure there is an acceptable substantiated rationale behind the changes being reflected. Further details on applying these performance and funding trends to decision-making can be found in Chapter 6 on using this information for budget formulation and Appendix A.

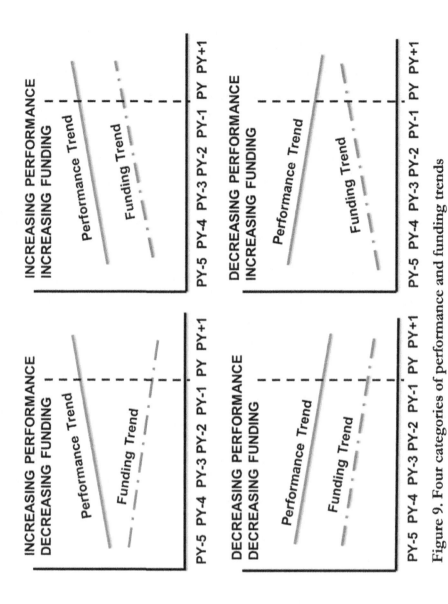

Figure 9. Four categories of performance and funding trends

While Figure 9 depicts performance and funding trends for single program areas one-at-a-time, an organization's senior leadership and management often need a more holistic approach to guiding an organization, to see how all the pieces are coming together to determine the best strategies for its overall success. Obtaining an organization-wide perspective on performance is challenging and time consuming considering the broad scope, number of program areas, and various activities needed to span a state or the nation. A scatterplot visualization, which displays performance and funding trends across multiple programs in a single exhibit, can provide an overview of the organization's performance. This approach is more compatible with the strategically-oriented perspectives of the senior leadership and management, helping them selectively determine where to best allocate their time across the total collection of the organization's activities.

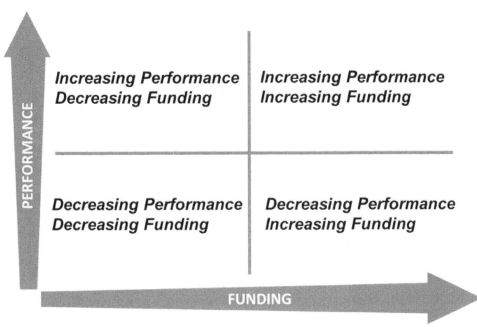

Figure 10. Integrating different categories of trends on single graph

In a scatterplot visualization, trends in performance and funding for each program area cover multiple past years for comparison with targets for the next two future planning years. Similar to the approach highlighted in Figure 9, senior leadership and management's attention is directed to whether or not performance and funding are increasing, staying the same, or decreasing. Senior leadership and management compare their expectations for each program area relative to the directions of these trends displayed in the scatterplot. As a result of this comparison, senior leadership and management will decide which program areas are most in need of further exploration and action. The trends in performance and funding are categorized into the same four categories of relationships discussed previously with Figure 9, but can now be plotted on the same chart in one of the following four quadrants, as in Figure 10 (Beck and O'Brien - 2015, 2018, 2019).

How the coordinates on the scatterplot, that reflect the performance and funding trends for each program area, are calculated is discussed further in Appendix B. A more detailed example for using the scatterplot visualization in budget formulation is provided in Chapter 6.

PRO: Comparing trends in performance and funding over multiple years provides an appropriate perspective to those program areas where results may take several years of funding and effort to be realized. Future projections and targets can be benchmarked against past actual experience and compared with senior leadership and management's expectations. Trends which are changing substantially are readily identifiable, and draw the user's attention to help confirm their consistency with planning or correcting an error in estimation. Areas of declining performance also draw the user's attention to considering their consistency with senior leadership and management's expectations for what they believe the organization should be working to accomplish.

Plotting the average changes in performance and funding from past history to future projections for multiple program areas on a scatterplot can afford senior leadership and management with an organization-wide perspective. This broad perspective across the organization's multiple components is more suitable to their holistic strategic role.

Using averages to plot the performance and funding trends on the scatterplot enables communication across a broader audience. This approach standardizes measurements despite the different sizes across program areas, and minimizes the complexity behind the construction of the scatterplot. As a result, the focus of discussion can be more about the observations from the scatterplot and the resulting effect on planning decisions, rather than wading through large volumes of data or trying to understand a complex calculation method.

CON: Some organizations may have difficulty estimating the funding associated with a key performance indicator. Similarly, they may not be comfortable associating the entire program budget with a key performance indicator. In the single program case (Figure 9), plotting performance and funding trends on the same graph will require different scales for the corresponding two Y-axes. The visual appearance of these two trend lines is dependent upon the increments used in each scale which are determined on a relatively subjective basis.

While some of the graphing concerns can be avoided when using the scatterplot approach, some organizations that have tried using this scatterplot visualization expressed the following concerns:

- The scatterplot may not adequately accommodate the differences in size and scope of government programs.
- The position of program areas on the scatterplot might be misinterpreted as a reflection of relative quality or priority of the programs.
- Observers will become obsessed with the relative magnitudes of the index values and draw incorrect conclusions.
- The organization is unable to allocate the amount of funding to each performance measure.

However, we believe the scatterplot visualization can be a tool for helping members of senior leadership and management strategically review performance and funding from an organization-wide perspective. As a visualization tool, the scatterplot is not meant to reflect all of reality's nuances, but rather provide a perspective to help focus further analysis and discussion. In realizing where less can be more (Principle #3), employing a more complete inventory of details in the visualization would complicate its use. Adding more data elements would likely be a deterrent, rather than an aid, to discussing performance information with senior leadership and management. The further details beyond the information provided in the scatterplot are meant to be pursued selectively, in a guided step-wise progression, rather than attempting to routinely review the full inventory of supporting details.

We hope that the scatterplot visualization could be employed as a modelling approximation to provide an overall perspective across multiple program areas. This overall perspective is more consistent with the strategic role of senior leadership and management, helping them better strategize across the organization. In providing an overall perspective, the scatterplot can help senior leadership and management allocate their time to those areas most in need of their particular attention and assistance, rather than reviewing the details across the entire collection of program areas.

Conducting routine performance status reviews

To be effective, these performance assessments need to be actively discussed, in accordance with Principles #1 and #2, directly among leadership, senior management, and the technical workforce. Performance status reviews, conducted quarterly and sometimes monthly, provide the opportunities to apply the key performance indicators and collectively determine if progress has been adequate or whether adjustments are needed to better ensure the timely achievement of the strategic objectives and goals.

Routinely conducted status reviews should be purposeful and action oriented, with direct participation by the managers responsible for conducting the program and senior leadership and management. This is not just a show-and-tell report. Status reviews should identify and address specific issues. Reviews that take too much time rehashing routine results can be considered a waste of time.

APPLICATION OF PRINCIPLES #1 (INVOLVEMENT) and #2 (ACTIVE MANAGEMENT): Involving senior leadership and management along with the technical workforce in regularly conducted status reviews exercises active management where progress and possible corrected actions are decided upon through direct collaboration.

Some questions for constructing a purposeful review could include:

- Have the recent key milestones been successfully accomplished or nearing completion? Are there any threats or concerns to accomplishing the next key milestones? (i.e., key milestones are those that are considered on the program's critical path, which if not accomplished on time impact achieving the program's final milestone for completion.)
- Is the program presently operating within its planned budget, i.e., on its planned spending-rate, and is that spending-rate supported for at least the remainder of the year? Are there any present threats to maintaining that spending-rate?
- How much of the reserves (for schedule or funding) has been spent and how much remains?
- What is the likelihood that each program will complete its strategic objectives and goals on-time and within-budget based on this recent progress assessment? If this likelihood is low, what is the issue, and is there a planned workaround or corrective action? Conducting this discussion during a status review can identify emerging problems and perhaps a solution that is developed collaboratively in advance of its impact. This improves the probability of achieving the strategic objectives and the goals, builds the organization's problem-solving

capability, and increases the workforce's involvement in achieving the organization's goal.

- Based on additional experience in actually executing the program, are there other changes to the activity that would better ensure its success; what and why?

- What assistance (resources and/or approvals) is needed from senior leadership and management to proceed with any proposed changes and the next phase?

Status reviews are conducted for the benefit of the organization. Proceedings should not become stuck on a single topic. If necessary, a follow-up meeting should be arranged to address that topic so that the entire agenda can be completed.

Level of detail should correspond with the level of management attending the review. In accordance with Principle #3, presentations should focus on providing the information that is most relevant to making decisions on next steps that better ensure success. Summary displays may be more useful than overwhelming the decision-makers with copious amounts of data. Senior leadership and management that span across multiple programs might appreciate relatively more comprehensive displays with aggregated information than trying to interpret too many separate data points. Their time should be spent on making the strategic decisions that are suitable to their position rather than making too many tactical decisions that are more suitable to an individual program manager.

APPLICATION OF PRINCIPLE #3 (LESS CAN BE MORE): For the continued involvement of senior leadership and management in status reviews, the level of detail should correspond with their level of responsibility. Presentations should focus on providing the information that is most relevant to their decision-making in terms of next steps and/or follow up actions that help better ensure overall success.

Action items should be created for unanswered/open questions and follow-up actions created during the status review. Each action item should identify:

- a due date, perhaps at the next status review or a follow-up meeting
- an individual responsible for the action's completion
- the recipient whose decision-making is most affected by the action's result

The review's materials, findings, and follow-up actions should be available on an easy-to-read website to educate other members of the organization beyond the status review's direct participants. This helps develop a community across the workforce which better understands the organization's efforts.

One primary rule for conducting status reviews is that all discussions should be conducted in a constructive manner. While problems will be discussed, all discussions should be conducted for the purpose of finding a resolution for the benefit of the program and hence the organization. If proceedings are too critical or considered likely to be punitive, participants will become hesitant to bring forth potentially bad news.

Some organizations began their practice of quarterly status reviews by focusing on Agency Priority Goals. Agency Priority Goals were codified in the Government Performance and Results Act (GPRA) Modernization Act of 2010 and have been used to focus on implementing new policies, improving a practice/process, or achieving a particular level of performance with a clear recognizable quantifiable target to be reached in two years. To better ensure the Agency Priority Goal is achieved on time, quarterly status reviews are conducted with the organization's senior leadership and management, and a designated goal leader. At these reviews, the goal leader provides a progress assessment relative to the plan that was established for the goal, a probability of success, and any potential corrective actions needed to better ensure success. Senior leadership and management's involvement in the quarterly review reinforces the importance of achieving the goal to the rest of the organization's managers and workforce, along with an opportunity to provide their assistance as needed. The creation and use of Agency Priority Goals are further discussed in Chapter 7.

Key Points

- An organization's success can be facilitated by tracking the interim progress toward its objectives and goals that were established in the Strategic Plan, using the corresponding performance measures. Tracking and assessing progress on an interim basis helps identify potential problems in advance so that corrective action can be taken to help minimize impacts and better ensure success.

- Routine plan vs. actual tracking – requires estimated levels of progress by each upcoming month, quarter, or year in producing commodities or benefits, to be compared with the actual level of progress achieved with each corresponding interval. The result of this comparison can help indicate whether alternative action is needed to better ensure success.

- Red/Yellow/Green assessment – provides a comprehensive assessment of an activity's progress and potential for future problems, including the extent of any problems (expected or realized), the likelihood of solving the problem, and the degree of assistance needed.

- Comparing performance and funding trends over multiple years – provides perspective on the investment of funding and the performance realized over time, since performance for many government programs may take more than one year to achieve results. This also helps benchmark future projections of performance and funding against past actual experience.

- Routinely conducted status reviews are essential for applying performance measures and assessment techniques in determining whether adequate progress is being made, probabilities for success, and possible alternatives where needed to help better ensure success.

- These status reviews should be attended by technical managers from the selected program along with senior leadership and management. The collaboration of the attendees can help the organization better ensure its success while developing working relationships and camaraderie across the organization.
- To be effective, routine status reviews should:
    - be action-oriented and purposeful, by addressing specific topics, issues, and/or questions that benefit the success of the organization;
    - be constructive and not punitive;
    - employ a level of detail corresponding with the management level of the decision-makers at the review;
    - use review materials developed and distributed prior to the meeting; and
    - assign follow-up actions to individuals with deadlines.

Chapter 6: Using Performance Information for Budget Formulation

Government programs require adequate funding to obtain the workforce, materials, equipment, and supporting infrastructure needed for achieving the organization's goals. Obtaining these resources requires the review and approval from the government chief executive officer and legislature (e.g., for federal agencies, this includes the President, the Office of Management and Budget, and Congress). The budget process for obtaining these funds can become quite complicated with:

- time allowed for planning, formulation, justification, and appropriation
- numerous contributors to each step of the decision process
- various analyses of progress, needs, and options

Navigating the government budget formulation process

The budget process involves multiple layers across the organization from unit managers to leadership, the government chief executive office (whether the White House, governor's office, or a city or county executive), and the legislature's subcommittees and budget committee.

Senior leadership and management take the lead role in overseeing the organization's budget planning, formulation, and justification. They rely upon support from the organization's budget office to work with the corresponding managers and administrative offices. The Strategic Plan, with its goals and strategic objectives, provides a reference source of what needs to be funded in the budget to fulfill the mission in accordance with the senior leadership's vision. Involving the technical workforce in formulating the budget can help input plausibility into the decisions determining the funding levels to be requested.

In addition to matching the goals and strategic objectives in the Strategic Plan, the funding requests proposed by the technical workforce will also need to be compared against the funding priorities and guidelines provided by the government chief executive's budget office. These guidelines may be somewhat restrictive due to balanced budget requirements and efforts to control government deficits. The organization's budget office assists senior leadership and management in assessing the various funding requests from the technical workforce relative to how to best achieve the organization's goals within the government chief executive's budget guidance. The technical workforce's involvement in adjusting their proposals to accommodate this guidance can help keep them engaged as active participants in addressing budget-related challenges and co-owners of the solutions ensuring the organization's continued health.

Sharing feedback on budget decisions needs to be carefully coordinated so as to not precede the government chief executive's formal budget announcement. The budget formulation process takes months for the various levels of management and leadership to review, offer input, negotiate, and determine the budget's final details. Iterations of the budget prior to receiving final chief executive office approval are considered pre-decisional or "budget sensitive," and are not to be discussed with the legislature or the public prior to formal release. Discussions with the legislature and the public should remain on the formal budget request rather than rehashing any previous interim drafts created during the formulation process. Maintaining focus on the formal budget request allows for a more organized discussion at the time that the budget proposal has been released, rather than revisiting any partial step in the formulation process during which details and rationale may have still been in development.

The outline of a generalized government budget formulation process is provided in Figure 11. A federal government organization can take 12 months to formulate its budget request to Congress, beginning in February of the year prior to the start of the budget year. Congress debates the budget requests submitted in the following February for the start of the budget year that October. The federal budget planning process typically includes:

73

- two months for senior leadership and management's initial determination of what to investigate during the budget process to ensure achievement of the organization's goals, while considering the government chief executive's budget guidance; this budget planning guidance is issued to the organization's programs and functions;
- two months for the organization's programs and functions to assess their progress in achieving objectives, determine any funding issues, and formulate their recommendations for submission back to senior leadership and management through the organization's budget office;
- two months for the organization's budget office to work with senior leadership and management in determining the content of the budget to be submitted to the government chief executive's budget office; budget proposals are assessed relative to achieving strategic plan goals and guidance from the government chief executive;
- one month to finalize and document the details justifying the organization's budget submission;
- four months for the government chief executive's budget office to review the organization's budget proposal and negotiate any adjustments consistent with the government chief executive's policy priorities; and
- one month to prepare final justifications and documentation to support the budget submission to the legislature.

Following the budget submission to Congress, there are at least seven months during which hearings and deliberations are conducted. These deliberations lead to formulating the appropriations for the upcoming budget year (i.e., present fiscal year + one year), which are provided to the President (government chief executive) for signature. For more information on the federal budget process, see Gessaman (2006).

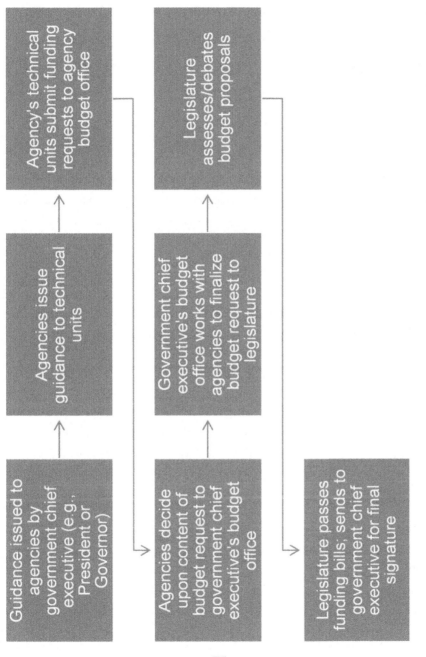

Figure 11. Outline of a typical government budget formulation process

State governments have similar steps in their budget formulation processes, potentially on different fiscal year timeframes from the federal government. Some states formulate budgets on a biennial basis and appropriate funds every two years. Budget amendments are passed during the years between the biennial appropriations to adjust funding if needed.

Tools for performance-informed budget planning

For many government programs, it can be more informative to compare the actual performance results and funding from the past 3-5 years vs. plans for the following two years (i.e., present year and the upcoming year). Considering the performance and funding over these multiple years can provide insight into the effects of unique or varying natural, social, economic, or political conditions on the organization's results from any particular year. The past historic levels of actual performance and funding can provide a benchmark against which projections of future funding and performance can be calibrated.

As discussed previously in Chapter 5, program areas can be categorized to determine those most in need of attention during the budget formulation process, as illustrated in Figure 9, by analyzing their trends in performance and funding over multiple years. These categories include:

- Increasing Performance and Decreasing Funding – requiring minimal attention
- Both Increasing (or Decreasing) Performance and Funding – confirm consistency with senior leadership and management's expectations
- Decreasing Performance and Increasing Funding – explore and determine if acceptable, and whether alternate actions are needed to increase performance

In Figure 12, a program providing assistance to various locations/sites is being reviewed for the fiscal year (FY) 2021 budget planning process. The number of sites improved after receiving assistance from the program are displayed on the graph, along with the corresponding level of funding. Data for years 2016 through 2020 depict actual past performance, while the data for the year 2021 include the present plans for the proposed 2021 Budget.

In this particular example, the decreasing trend in performance appears to begin responding to the increased funding provided in 2019 and 2020, with a level of 174 improved sites in 2020 which is higher than the previous two years. With a similar level of performance planned for 2021, estimating 170 sites to be improved, a decision to level-off the funding at $38M would appear sensible. Yet, the overall 2021 performance percentage of 34% is much less than the prior 75-85% level of achievement. Notice that while the numerator of the metric, i.e., number of sites improved, is staying somewhat level, the total number of sites requesting assistance, i.e., the denominator of the metric, more than doubles relative to prior experience. The question for the budget planners is whether this substantial increase in sites requesting assistance is reasonable and feasible to address with the same level of funding? If not, the senior leadership and management may need to provide additional funds, either as an augmentation or transfer from another program. However, the much lower level of sites requesting assistance over the past five years, makes the 2021 projection suspicious of possibly being overstated. The validity of the 2021 projection needs to be further explored so that an effective decision can be made on whether additional funding to achieve the proposed higher target is warranted. The information provided in Figure 12 brings attention to this question that is important to formulating the budget.

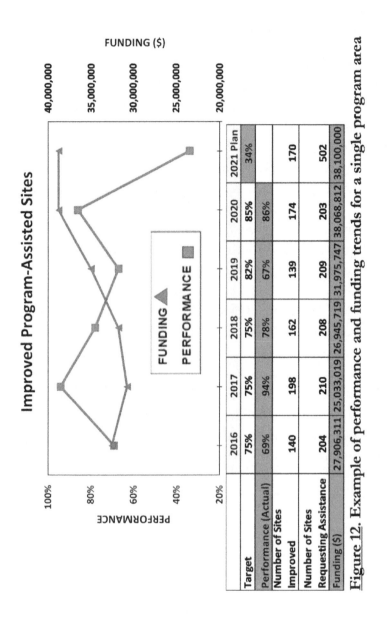

	2016	2017	2018	2019	2020	2021 Plan
Target	75%	75%	75%	82%	85%	34%
Performance (Actual)	69%	94%	78%	67%	86%	
Number of Sites Improved	140	198	162	139	174	170
Number of Sites Requesting Assistance	204	210	208	209	203	502
Funding ($)	27,906,311	25,033,019	26,945,719	31,975,747	38,068,812	38,100,000

Figure 12. Example of performance and funding trends for a single program area

While the technique presented in Figure 12 can be used to assess performance and funding trends for one program area at a time, an organization's senior

78

leadership and management would need to review several of these charts to assess performance and funding across the organization's full cadre of programs (i.e., agencies can easily have as many as 200 programs). As introduced in Chapter 5, a scatterplot can be constructed to plot the performance and funding trends of multiple program areas on a single chart, providing a strategic perspective that is more commensurate with the needs of senior leadership and management. The scatterplot reflects performance and funding trends as the change from the past to what is projected for the future.

Figure 13 provides an example of the percent change in average annual performance and funding plotted for a collection of government health programs, based on data provided in Appendix B. Rather than participating in a detailed review of all eight programs, the organization's leadership and senior management attention would be more immediately drawn to:

- confirming that the programs in the lower left quadrant (decreasing performance and funding) on drinking water improvement projects (H1) and shellfish safety (H4) are consistent with leadership's priorities; and

- ensuring that the programs in the lower right quadrant (decreasing performance with increasing funding) on health insurance assistance (H7) and community treatment centers (H8) are being adequately funded and managed, or need adjustment to increase performance.

In this way, the information provided in Figure 13 can assist senior leadership and management in their use of performance information to guide their budget formulation activities. Further details on the use of this scatterplot visualization are provided in Appendix B.

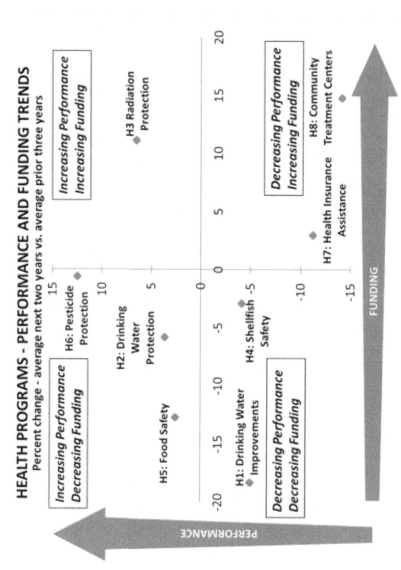

Figure 13. Performance and funding trends for multiple programs on a single display

Organize budget decisions into three tiers

Senior leadership and management develop the organization's budget request by balancing the needs for ensuring the achievement of the goals in the Strategic Plan with political affordability. Developing a budget that can be traced to achieving the organization's strategic objectives and goals in the Strategic Plan is reassuring to executive and legislative budget decision-makers. Traceability to the Strategic Plan confirms that the organization is continuing to follow the same path which was previously discussed with them.

Political affordability is determined by comparing the organization's budget request against the target levels provided by the government chief executive's budget office; e.g., target funding levels for federal government budget planning are provided by the Office of Management and Budget on behalf of the President. Along with reflecting the chief executive's policy priorities for an agency, the budget target level issued to the agency often reflects a portion of what is considered to be affordable for the entire government to spend. In estimating how much the government can afford to spend, the benefits to be produced are considered against the effect on the economy, the ability of the government to borrow money, and the corresponding size of the public debt. Therefore, if an organization requests more funding than was allocated in the budget target level it was provided, there can be a ripple effect impacting the allocations issued to other agencies in order to maintain the planned government-wide total budget.

Hence there is pressure on the organization to remain within its issued budget target level. The organization needs to strategize what it could adjust or delete to accommodate the target level. Any requests above the target level must be carefully considered and crafted. How the organization addresses the target level in its budget request affects its credibility and the ability to obtain the funding necessary for achieving its mission. A stepwise three-tier process can be used to organize these options for discussion and decision.

KEY CONCEPT: Senior leadership and management decide upon the budget's content by balancing what is needed to ensure the achievement of the goals defined in its strategic plan, and political affordability.

Being able to trace the organization's budget to achieving its previously stated strategic objectives and goals reassures executive and legislative decision-makers that the organization is continuing to follow the plan they had previously discussed with them.

In response to the guidance provided by senior leadership and management, the technical and functional units in the organization assess their funding requirements for achieving the strategic objectives and submit recommendations to the organization's budget office. The budget office reviews the requests and separates the suitable requests from those that appear impractical, unsubstantiated, and/or fail to meet the organization's guidance. The budget office provides to senior leadership and management its assessment of the options that have the best potential for achieving the organization's goals within the present programmatic, technical, and political conditions. Deciding upon the content of the organization's budget request can be assisted by reviewing, discussing, and deciding upon budget proposals using three tiers as in Figure 14:

- Tier 1: Maintaining existing programs within the organization's presently approved total budget level (i.e., baseline budget)
- Tier 2: Augmentations to existing programs
- Tier 3: New initiatives and opportunities.

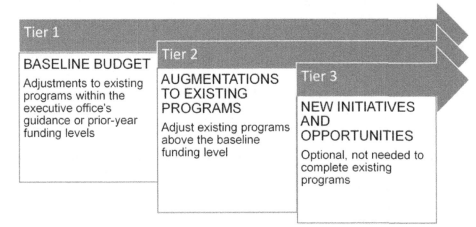

Tier 1

BASELINE BUDGET

Adjustments to existing programs within the executive office's guidance or prior-year funding levels

Tier 2

AUGMENTATIONS TO EXISTING PROGRAMS

Adjust existing programs above the baseline funding level

Tier 3

NEW INITIATIVES AND OPPORTUNITIES

Optional, not needed to complete existing programs

<u>Figure 14</u>. Organize budget decisions into three tiers.

Tier 1: Baseline Budget - Maintaining existing approved programs

The first tier of decision-making is focused on determining the content of existing programs for achieving the Strategic Plan with no additional funding to the organization's formally approved total budget level. This could include the budget target level provided by the government chief executive's budget office, or a repeat of the previous year's appropriation level (if lacking executive guidance). This is considered the "within-budget" or baseline budget funding scenario for delivering on the organization's existing commitments.

Tier 1 baseline budget decisions include identifying adjustments to program content, schedules, workforce, workload, and/or capabilities needed to maintain the present cadre of approved programs for executing the Strategic Plan within the baseline budget funding level. This includes addressing shortcomings or problems which impose a threat on successfully conducting a program. Shortcomings could include higher than anticipated costs of labor, materials, utilities, or money (i.e., inflation), etc. Problems could include technical issues, e.g., designs that do not work in practice, execution errors, etc., preferably previously identified in status reviews (as discussed in Chapter 5). These all need to be considered within the baseline budget target level provided by the government chief executive's budget office.

Organizations need to consider potential adjustments to operate within existing funding levels as government chief executives and/or legislators may be unable to add additional funding when balancing budgets and/or reducing government debt. A list of possible zero-sum changes in order to maintain the within-baseline budget level can include the following:

- reduce or flatline workforce levels;
- expand the amount of time to complete a project or deliver services;
- defer starting any new, previously approved activities that are not already underway;
- eliminate any activities that can't be clearly linked to a goal documented in the Strategic Plan and authorizing legislation;
- economize acquisitions of materials and technical support across organizational units;
- consider sharing administrative and operational activities across units within, and external to the organization;
- close and eliminate underutilized facilities, increase reliance on shared and/or leased facilities;
- ensure a paying customer for multiprogram support; e.g., some agencies have found IT networks, test capabilities, or cadres of technical subject matter experts that are routinely budgeted without identified customers; and
- contract for support from outside sources rather than maintain internal capabilities where less costly from a full cost perspective.

The changes to schedules, levels of workforce, and performance associated with maintaining the organization's existing programs within the baseline budget's funding level should be provided to the government chief executive budget office as part of the budget request. In this way, it is clear as to what adjustments the organization is making to fund its existing approved activities within the baseline budget level.

Tier 2: Augmentations to existing programs

Once the Tier 1 within-baseline budget scenario has been determined, the organization's senior leadership and management can then decide if they want to propose any augmentations to the existing programs. In requesting additional funding, emphasis should be placed on describing why each augmentation is of high priority to achieving a particular strategic objective and goal, the factors driving the need for the augmentation, and what benefits to the constituency would be delayed or deferred without the augmentation.

Provide background information from the status reviews such as higher-than-anticipated costs outside the control of the program, any technical issues, and any plans for improving the probability of success. The particular importance for the augmentation could be aided by a time-critical factor for conducting the activity. This second tier considers augmentations to only existing approved programs. New initiatives should be considered separately in the third tier of the budget planning decision process.

Tier 3: New Initiatives and Opportunities

With decisions completed for the first two tiers of budget planning, the organization's senior leadership and management now have a sense of what is most needed in the budget request to continue toward achieving their vision for the organization. At this point, candidates for new initiatives can be considered using the following guidelines:

- The proposed initiative is separate from the completion of any existing approved programs. If the proposed new initiative is not approved, there will be no impact to an existing program.
- There are clearly described benefits to the community that would otherwise not be realized.

Following these three tiers of decisions, the organization now has the components of its budget request to be submitted to the government chief executive. This three-tier approach organizes budget decision-making into a stepwise process where ensuring existing commitments take priority. Augmentations and especially new initiatives are presented as opportunities rather than demands. Applying these categories provide budget proposals with a more appealing perspective, hopefully inviting a more constructive than confrontational discussion and promoting more thoughtful consideration by the government chief executive for subsequent submission to the legislature.

This stepwise three-tier decision-making process still relies upon the senior leadership and management's judgement, often aided by the budget office's experience and analysis, of how receptive the government chief executive and legislature will be to requests for more funding. Even if the requests for augmentations and new initiatives are rejected, this planning process still provides a budget plan for achieving the organization's vision, even if on a modified approach and/or schedule.

Creating budget justifications

Most often, the formats for submitting budget justifications are defined by the government chief executive's budget office and/or the legislature's sub-committee which receive them. However, as part of these materials be sure to provide the following information to help strengthen the organization's budget request.

Budget justification materials should include an explanation of how the requested funding will help achieve the strategic objectives and accomplish the goals described in the Strategic Plan. Identify the corresponding program, and amount of funding contributing to the achievement of each strategic objective and goal. This demonstrates that the proposed budget is consistent with achieving the plan that was established by the organization and previously discussed with its chief executive and legislative stakeholders. This consistency fosters credibility with stakeholders, as a demonstration of the organization's continuing commitment to produce the benefits documented in the Strategic Plan. This becomes a stronger argument for supporting the budget request when the technical workforce is involved in finalizing the Strategic Plan, including developing, targeting, and reporting its performance measures and the initial budget requests.

Clearly identify the benefits to be achieved by the organization's use of the funding being requested. Be as specific as possible. Do not simply state that conditions will be "better." Use the organization's performance measures that were developed with the Strategic Plan to report progress toward achieving the strategic objectives. Provide estimates of what can be achieved in the future using the performance measures' targets in context of the past 3-5 years of experience. Be sure that the technical workforce, who provide the performance measure targets, base the future targets on the amount of funding being requested in the budget, not the budget they personally consider most likely to be appropriated. Also be sure to highlight key performance indicators that can represent potential achievements at the organizational level. In accordance with Principle #3, the budget's audience is more likely to appreciate reading about a descriptive snapshot or summary of potential results across programs using key performance indicators than being overwhelmed by numerous raw data points.

APPLICATION OF PRINCIPLE #3 (LESS CAN BE MORE): A budget proposal's audience is more likely to appreciate reading about a descriptive snapshot of potential results across programs using key performance indicators than being overwhelmed by numerous raw data points.

Key points

- The organization's senior leadership and management use the budget formulation, justification, and appropriation process to obtain the funding and operating authorities necessary for realizing their vision.

- The government budget formulation process is quite lengthy and involves several phases of review and approval by:
  - the organization's technical units submitting funding proposals to senior leadership and management;
  - the government chief executive; and
  - the legislature leading to appropriation.
- The Strategic Plan provides a means for judging which proposals should be included in the organization's budget request, by specifying the strategic objectives to be achieved and the goals to be accomplished necessary for realizing the organization's vision.
- Even though budgets are submitted and approved on either an annual or biennial basis, budget planning can be facilitated by comparing the funding and performance trends over multiple years.
- Deciding on the content of the organization's budget request can be facilitated by using a stepwise three-tier process:
  - adjustments to existing programs needed to stay within the baseline budget;
  - potential augmentations needed for existing programs; and
  - optional new opportunities that are independent of completing any existing programs.
- The organization's budget request should include clear descriptions of the funding's relevance to achieving the strategic objectives and goals in the Strategic Plan.

Chapter 7: Agency Priority Goals – Targeting Specific Areas for Success

Operational Description

The Government Performance and Results Act (GPRA) Modernization Act (Public Law 111-352) provides a tool for mobilizing an organization's efforts to successfully achieve specially identified goals of importance. These special goals are referred to as Agency Priority Goals, which should have the following characteristics:

- limited in number (perhaps 2-4);
- reflect an area of importance for senior leadership and management, related to a goal in the organization's Strategic Plan;
- contain a quantifiable target that the public recognizes as beneficial, to be achieved in two years' time; and
- a specific individual held responsible for accomplishing the goal and reporting interim progress to senior leadership and the public quarterly.

Agency Priority Goals are not meant to cover all of the organization's activities but rather focus on specific areas of particular importance to the organization's senior leadership and management. They have been especially useful in providing added emphasis to creating and/or implementing a new activity, or changing a prior practice or process to improve or correct performance.

These goals should be defined in clear, recognizable, and quantifiable terms. As we have discussed, past experience has demonstrated the motivational value of a clearly defined goal (Kohli, 2010). With a clearly defined goal, the workforce understand what they are working toward producing, and what leadership expects of them. Working toward a clear goal provides a focus for their efforts with a definitive target to be achieved. Some examples of Agency Priority Goals are provided in Table 4 from the www.performance.gov website. Notice the descriptiveness of the goal statement, the quantification of the two-year target, and the relatively high level within the organization of the goal leader responsible for its implementation and reporting to senior leadership and management.

Table 4. Examples of Agency Priority Goals

Agency Priority Goal Statement	Two-year target	Goal Leader/Agency
Protect Families from Lead-Based Paint and Other Health Hazards	Make an additional 23,500 at-risk housing units healthy and lead-safe by the end of FY 2018-2019.	Director of the Office of Lead Hazard Control and Healthy Homes, Department of Housing and Urban Development
Water Conservation and Supply Enhancement	By the end of FY 2020-2021, the Bureau of Reclamation will facilitate water conservation capacity of 114,108 acre-feet.	Commissioner, Bureau of Reclamation (BOR)
Strengthen Federal Cybersecurity	By the end of FY 2020-2021, 75% of critical and high configuration-based vulnerabilities identified through high value asset assessments will be mitigated within 30 days.	Deputy Director, Cybersecurity and Infrastructure Security Agency, Department of Homeland Security

Routine Status Reviews

Conducting routine quarterly status reviews is an important characteristic of Agency Priority Goals. These reviews provide an opportunity to consider the level of progress relative to the previously devised plan, and the priority goal leader's estimated probability for achieving success by the end of the two-year period. This probability does not necessarily have to be provided in terms of a percentage. The goal leader can provide an estimated likelihood for achieving the goal on schedule in terms of low, medium, or high, along with a corresponding rationale for the projection.

Since this assessment is being provided directly to the organization's senior leadership and management, we would expect the goal leader will be as forthcoming and informative as possible in providing an accurate forecast and identifying any potential problems. Bringing possibly bad news should not be punished unless it had been withheld or reflects negligence. What could be considered bad news should be considered in constructive terms of finding alternative corrections, workarounds, or other means for improving probabilities of success. Providing an understanding of the interfering factors and possible corrective actions demonstrate technical and managerial expertise. Such a demonstration of the organization's capabilities can help bolster its credibility for pursuing the goal although the milestone was missed.

Senior leadership and management's participation in the quarterly reviews facilitates their potential assistance in those matters that are beyond the authorities of the goal leader. This collaboration is an exercise of active management, per Principle #2. Their participation also reinforces the importance of achieving the goal to the organization and its continued pursuit. The information presented for each Agency Priority Goal should be limited to that which helps senior leadership and management readily understand the extent of progress, estimated probability for success, and any potential problems requiring their assistance. As senior leadership and management involvement is necessary for success, this more strategic streamlined approach can promote their continued participation in the review process, as per Principle #3.

APPLICATION OF PRINCIPLE #2 (ACTIVE MANAGEMENT): The direct collaboration among the senior leadership, management, and technical workforce provides for a more effective exchange of policy and implementation information. This can improve the probability of successfully achieving the goal.

APPLICATION OF PRINCIPLE #3 (LESS IS MORE): The information for each Agency Priority Goal should be limited to that which helps senior leadership and management readily understand the extent of progress, estimated probability for success, and any potential problems requiring their assistance. As senior leadership and management involvement is necessary for success, this streamlined approach can help ensure their continued engagement.

When properly conducted, Agency Priority Goals afford the organization a method for increasing its chances for success in attaining the selected two-year goals, assuming the goals are defined in clear terms recognizable to the workforce and the public, and senior leadership and management are involved. An Agency Priority Goal does not necessarily need to be continued or renewed after its initial two-year period. For those Agency Priority Goals that are successful in institutionalizing a new activity, or establishing a new more preferred level of achievement for a particular activity, the organization's senior leadership and management could select another area of change or improvement as a new Agency Priority Goal to emphasize for the next 2 years. In this way, Agency Priority Goals can be used selectively on a rotational basis to highlight particular areas targeted for improvement.

Key points

- Creating and implementing Agency Priority Goals can help improve the probabilities for successfully achieving specially targeted activities.

- Agency Priority Goals help provide added emphasis on especially challenging activities that create and/or implement a new activity, change a prior practice to improve or correct performance, or achieve a particular level of performance for a specified case.
- To be effective, Agency Priority Goals:
    - are limited in number;
    - are identified by senior leadership and management as an achievement that is important to them;
    - specify a clear quantifiable target to be achieved in two years that is readily recognizable as valuable by the workforce and the public;
    - identify a specific individual responsible for achieving the goal and regularly reporting progress to senior leadership and management;
    - include continued involvement, and potential assistance, by the organization's senior leadership and management in the goal's progress; and
    - are regularly reviewed and publicly reported on a quarterly basis to assess progress, probability for success, and need for any alternative actions to better ensure success.
- Information presented at quarterly status reviews should be tailored to the needs and decision levels of senior leadership and management to facilitate their participation and ensure their continued involvement in the Agency Priority Goal process.
- Agency Priority Goals can be used on a rotating basis to highlight particular areas for achievement during a two-year timeframe. Once a goal is achieved in a sustainable manner, another area for potential improvement can be selected for emphasis and attention during the next two-year timeframe.

Chapter 8: Organizational Considerations for Effective Performance Management

The following describes the essential roles and skills needed within an organization for implementing the processes presented in this book for effective performance management. Characteristics are described for the following essential roles:

- senior leadership
- senior management
- organization-wide performance analysts
- specialized technical experts
- administrative, management, and technical support

Senior leadership

Senior leadership need to provide the vision that defines the organization's purpose and direction, i.e., what benefits should be provided to its constituency. A Strategic Plan Framework can help organize the senior leadership's vision into the structure of a mission statement, goals, and strategic objectives used to develop the Strategic Plan. The Strategic Plan Framework can then be used to communicate the senior leadership's vision to senior management and the technical workforce. Senior management and the technical workforce provide their advice by aligning their capabilities to the corresponding goals through strategic objectives and offering technical adjustments to the goals where necessary.

The senior leadership needs to be willing to participate in assessing the interim progress using the performance measures developed and maintained by the organization's technical workforce. Senior leadership's involvement in reviewing progress (Principle #1) emphasizes to the technical workforce the importance of achieving the goals and their willingness to assist as needed.

It is important to remember that senior leadership also has a significant up-and-out role in securing effective working relationships and arrangements with other organizations; attaining legislative support for authorizations and appropriations; ensuring support from constituencies; and maintaining appropriate support from the government's chief executive. These are the senior leadership's strategic roles and need to be considered in the extent and format of performance-related information provided to them that best assists their efforts and maintains their involvement.

APPLICATION OF PRINCIPLE #1 (INVOLVEMENT): The senior leadership needs to be willing to participate in assessing the interim progress using the performance measures developed and maintained by the organization's technical workforce. Senior leadership's participation in reviewing progress emphasizes to the technical workforce the importance of achieving the goals and their willingness to assist as needed.

Senior management

In our combined top-down/bottom-up discussion of Chapter 2, organizational theorists told us that dividing work among several specialized technical units is more beneficial to producing results than maintaining an organization of generalists. The specialized units are better able to each develop their own particular skills rather than a generalist attempting to perform multiple skills. Senior management can help organize and coordinate the technical contributions from the various specialized units to help ensure that goals are achieved.

With an understanding of the various technical units and the roles they play in realizing the vision, senior management can also offer adjustments to the goals and strategic objectives in the Strategic Plan Framework to bring the organization's aspirations in-line with its technical capabilities. Senior management may recognize a need to adjust the types and/or levels of technical capabilities in the organization, through the budget process, human resources hiring, or acquisition process to better ensure that goals are attained.

Senior management positions are very valuable for connecting the more specialized technical experts with the overarching organization-wide and policy perspectives of the organization's senior leadership. This is where the top-down meets bottom-up, connecting the technical means of the organization with its purpose. Senior management can help provide to the technical workforce the broader perspective of how their program or project contributes to the nation, or the state. Understanding this connection can be very motivational, so the technical experts better understand the value of their work and contributions to the overall organization on a national or statewide scale. Seeing where their work contributes to the organization and beyond can help develop a further sense of ownership in the organization's existence and future, per Principle #1.

APPLICATION OF PRINCIPLE #1 (INVOLVEMENT): Senior management positions are very valuable for connecting the more specialized technical experts with the overarching organization-wide and policy perspectives of the senior leadership. Helping the technical workforce see where they contribute can help develop a further sense of ownership in the organization's existence and future.

Organization-wide performance analysts

To effectively employ the methods discussed in this book for realizing a vision using performance management, a collection of specially-skilled analysts are needed to advise the senior leadership and management and guide the technical workforce in planning and performance methods. These individuals have the ability to understand the technical complexities of the various programs and functions, assess their progress, and determine the corresponding probability of success. These performance analysts understand and review how the various programs and functions collectively contribute to the organization's success, while relying on the technical experts for further details as needed. The organization's senior leadership and management do not have the time to collect, integrate, process, and assess all the individual implementation details themselves. Their attention is on the organization as a whole in achieving the overall mission. The performance analysts select the subset of key performance indicators that are most informative to the senior leadership and management for assessing progress and the probabilities for success from an organizational-wide perspective, per Principle #3. This helps senior leadership and management apply their time to where they are most needed and best suited to benefit the entire organization.

These performance analysts help senior leadership and management see the forest for the trees. For example, they may follow the critical path in a project schedule more than all its individual components as would a program or project manager. This involves tracking key major milestones as signals of progress and determining potential problems. Such analysts have the insight and talent to construct and use key performance indicators, or index values, such as the Gross Domestic Product to judge economic performance, or the Facility Condition Index (i.e., a ratio of the maintenance cost relative to the replacement value) to judge if a facility should be replaced rather than repaired. Using such indicators, analysts review performance across the scope of an organization's range of programs, helping guide the management of its activities.

These organization-wide performance analysts can help assemble the displays for quarterly status reviews, assess the appropriateness of annual performance targets submitted by the technical workforce for approval by senior leadership and management, or prepare the performance and funding trend scatterplot that provides an organization-wide perspective to senior leadership and management. Some organizations possess a dedicated planning and performance division which focuses on conducting the assessment, processing, and review activities discussed in this book. Other organizations integrate these activities into their budget offices with either dedicated individuals for planning and performance, or as additional tasks for each budget or program analyst. Combining performance and budgeting responsibilities in the same office can help better ensure that performance is considered in budget planning. However, increasing pressures on defending government spending and working greater quantities of budget options could impact an analyst's ability to collect, process, and analyze performance data. A dedicated performance analysis staff would have more time to focus on understanding the progress of programs and functions, analyze corresponding data to determine the prospects for future success, and determine where added attention is needed to better ensure goals are achieved. A dedicated performance analysis staff can function without the burdens of formulating budget options, preparing budget justification documents, and responding to what seems like a continuing parade of funding-related inquiries.

APPLICATION OF PRINCIPLE #3 (LESS CAN BE MORE): The performance analysts select the subset of key performance indicators that are most informative to senior leadership and management for assessing progress and the probabilities for success from an organizational-wide perspective. This helps senior leadership and management apply their time to where they are most needed and best suited to benefit the entire organization.

A more complete list of competencies for performance analysts is included in Appendix C, based on research that was conducted by the U.S. Office of Personnel Management during 2011. The competencies with their definition were provided in a memorandum from the Office of Personnel Management Director to federal government Chief Human Capital Officers, that was dated January 3, 2012.

Specialized technical experts

The organization's technical workforce is on the front line to implement and deliver the strategic objectives that achieve the goals necessary to accomplish the senior leadership's mission and realize their vision. Their specialized expertise, skills, and experience, implement programs and functions effectively and produce results that benefit the organization's constituencies. Here is the realization of the organization's existence, where its activities meet recipient. The technical managers and experts demonstrate their progress by reporting on performance measures that are meaningful to them. These measures represent their efforts and provide insight into the probability of success when compared to the plan they developed. Their performance measures are used in status reviews conducted regularly with senior leadership and management. This provides an opportunity for active management per Principle #2 where senior leadership and management hear about the status of implementation from the technical workforce, and directly work any necessary alternatives to better ensure success.

APPLICATION OF PRINCIPLE #2 (ACTIVE MANAGEMENT): In regularly conducted status reviews, senior leadership and management hear about the status of implementation from the technical workforce, and directly work any needed alternatives to better ensure success.

Administrative, management, and technical support

The administrative, management, and technical support personnel enable the effective implementation of programs. These experts provide guidance in effective business operations and resources to the organization's units. This guidance includes assisting with funding, skilled workforce, financial accountability, information technology, specialized technical assistance, and acquisition. The implementation of these functions is standardized as much as feasible across the organization, and comparable to other government organizations with similar mission characteristics. This minimizes confusion and the time needed to apply these capabilities across organizational units, rather than reinvent similar practices that have already been proven effective in other organizations.

Key points

To ensure effective performance management in helping achieve a vision, the following roles and skills are needed:

- senior leadership with a vision and a willingness to participate in routine progress assessments and determine where alternative action may be needed;
- senior management that is willing and capable of aligning technical capabilities with the visionary goals;
- performance analysts with an organization-wide perspective, analytical skills, and managerial expertise to guide and support effective planning and performance management;
- specialized technical experts for managing and implementing programs and functions; and
- administrative, management, and technical support who help enable the implementation of programs through effective business processes, operations, and adequate resources where needed; these activities include budget formulation, acquisition, human capital, financial management, information technology, etc.

Chapter 9: Summary - Is This All Worth It? What's Next?

This book provides a practical guide for establishing a system of planning and performance processes in an organization to help achieve the vision conceived by its senior leadership and management. These processes are the tools for helping exercise strategic leadership throughout the organization.

Review of tools

Tools provided in this book include:

- Guiding principles that promote a collaborative and engaged workforce, assist executive decision-making, and improve the organization's probabilities of success:
  - o Principle #1: Facilitate involvement across the organization;
  - o Principle #2: Exercise active rather than passive management; and
  - o Principle #3: Realize where less can be more.
- Methods for creating a Strategic Plan Framework to:
  - o help formulate and communicate senior leadership and management's vision, in terms of mission and goals;
  - o provide the means for the technical workforce to confirm the practicality of achieving the organization's goals, by aligning their capabilities with the vision through strategic objectives; and
  - o increase the technical workforce's sense of ownership in the organization's vision and improve their motivation to assist its accomplishment.
- A logic model to ensure the organization's abilities to successfully achieve its goals:
  - o aligns the appropriate resources, processes, and strategies for fulfilling each corresponding goal; and
  - o identifies gaps in resources, processes, or strategies to be added.
- Method for developing effective performance measures to track interim progress.

- Techniques for conducting routine interim performance status reviews to identify and resolve potential problem issues in advance of serious impact to the program.
- Methods for examining trends in the level of performance relative to the level of funding across the organization; assisting senior leadership and management's use of performance information in collaboration with the technical workforce.
- A stepwise process for deciding upon the content of the organization's budget proposal.
- Use of Agency Priority Goals to facilitate the achievement of highly desired areas of change or improvement through increased focus, use of strategically selected data, and regular interactive review by senior leadership, management, and technical workforce.
- Description of the roles and skills needed to implement effective performance management in an organization.

Is This All Worth It?

The performance management processes in this book can help an organization's senior leadership, management, and technical workforce develop a Strategic Plan, measure progress, anticipate potential problems, and formulate budgets. Implementing these processes provide several benefits.

For senior leadership and management:

- ability to develop and share a vision;
- ability to align the organization's resources and capabilities toward achieving the vision;
- means to engage the technical workforce toward achieving the vision;
- methods to obtain insight into the interim progress being made across the organization, to foresee potential problems and take corrective action prior to sizeable impact on achieving results;
- tools to formulate a budget to help realize the vision;

- methods to improve credibility with, and support from stakeholders and constituents; and
- methods to improve probability of realizing the vision.

For the technical workforce:

- a better understanding of the organization's purpose, as defined by the senior leadership and management's vision for what the organization should accomplish, and how each individual's efforts contribute to achieving the organization's overall mission and success;
- an increased sense of ownership in the organization's mission, performance, and accomplishments; and
- an increased sense of personal satisfaction through meaningful contribution to determining the organization's purpose.

For external stakeholders and constituents:

- a documented description of the organization's mission and its approach to achieving success in terms of trackable goals, strategic objectives, and performance measures; this information demonstrates the organization's managerial and technical competence, and maturity of thinking;
- evidence that the organization has taken the time and effort to decide on its future path, and is willing to ensure its success by using a predefined set of criteria to regularly review its progress, make adjustments, and report publicly; and
- a demonstration of the organization's credibility and justification for their continued support.

What's Next?

What's next depends upon the reader to apply these processes into his/her organization, using their vision, mission, goals, objectives, key performance indicators, and data. Employing these processes can help engage the workforce in utilizing performance measures to help achieve the strategic objectives and goals that realize the organization's vision. Hopefully the principles and processes presented in this book will serve the reader well in developing a collaborative and productive organization that provides valuable benefits to its constituency. Benefitting the constituency, i.e., the public, is the purpose of government organizations. An organization's ability to serve its constituency depends upon its leadership to guide and support the corresponding technical expertise by applying the processes and resources that enable its success.

The following flow chart (Figure 15) displays how the performance management processes presented in this book can be implemented as a "system" in the organization. For each major process, the key participants are identified along with an estimated time for conducting the process. The times for each process may vary depending upon the size of the organization, the number of units (i.e., programs and functions), and the extent of coordination needed. We wish you the best in applying these processes, achieving results, and your organization's success!

If you'd like to learn more, or share your experiences in implementing the processes and practices discussed in this book, please contact us at richbeckphd@outlook.com. Your experiences could help inform future editions of this book.

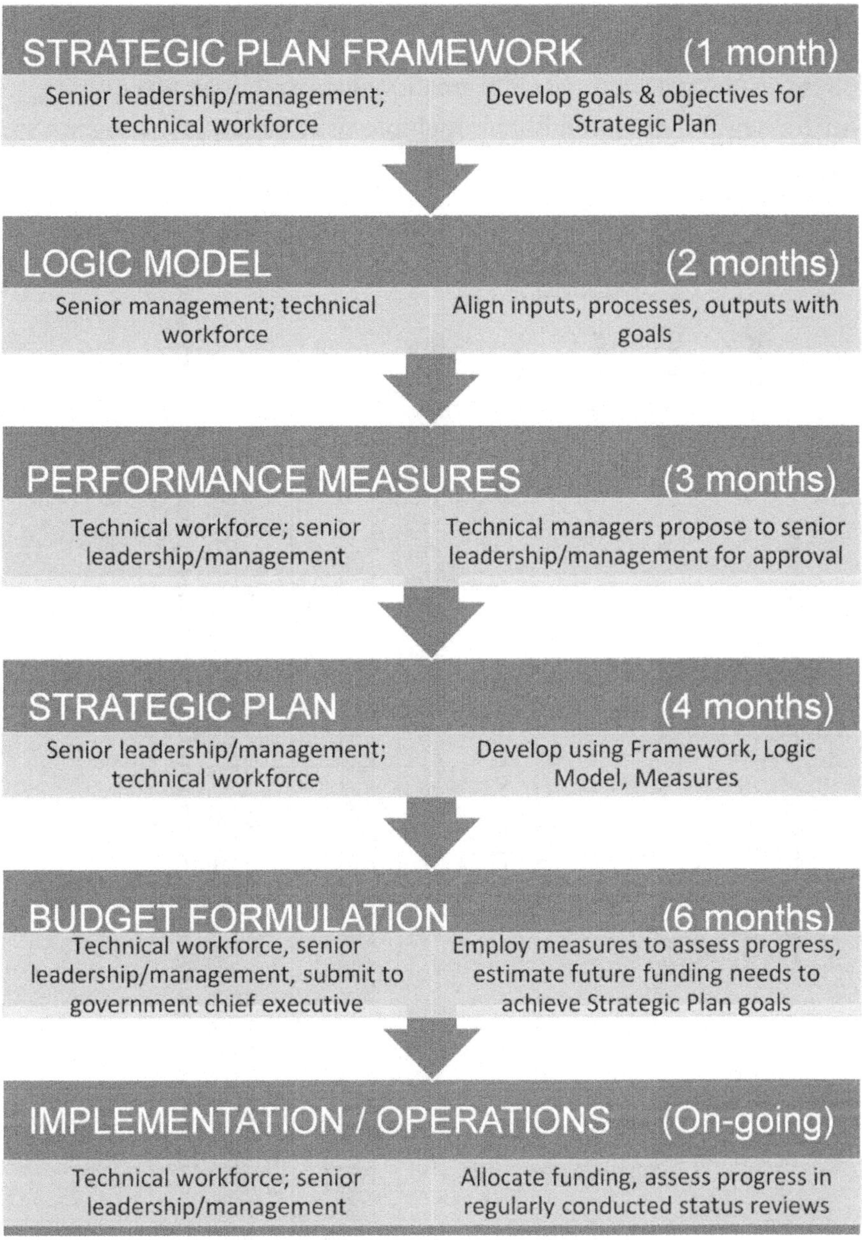

Figure 15. Flow chart of planning and performance management processes

Appendix A: Single Program Area Trend Analysis

The following illustrates how the information displayed in graphs of performance and funding trends over multiple years for a single program area from Figure 12 can be applied.

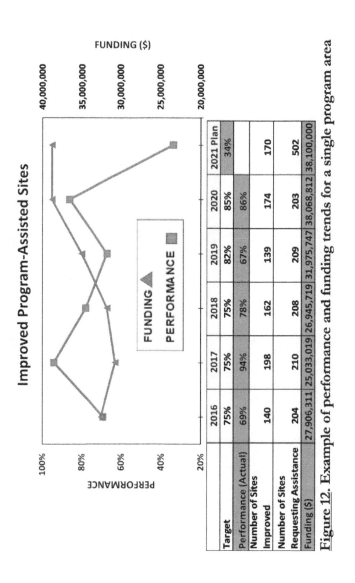

Figure 12. Example of performance and funding trends for a single program area

Compare the performance and funding trends over time and relative to each other.

- The years from 2016-2020 reflect "Actual" experience while 2021 is a "Plan" (projection or target) for the upcoming or present year. The actual years can provide a benchmark from which to compare/calibrate the targets for the present or future years.
- Past performance has been an average of 163 sites improved annually, ranging from 139 to 198. Funding has recently increased from approximately $27M per year (average for 2016, 2017, and 2018), to approximately $32M per year in 2019 and $38M per year in 2020 and 2021. Therefore, the program appears to have an increasing trend in funding.
- The fluctuation in sites improved annually indicates that some sites may take more than one year to demonstrate success.

Why is the 2021 performance target much lower than prior years' experience?

- The potential lower performance level in 2021 appears to be primarily due to the increase in the number of sites requesting assistance (the denominator of the percentage used for the performance metric) from 203 to 502. The corresponding number of assisted sites improved remains effectively constant, potentially due to maintaining the same level of funding from the prior year.

Based on its past experience, could the decreasing performance trend in 2021 reflect a program weakness or deficiency?

- The basis for the estimated 502 case applications in 2021 should be reviewed, especially since that level is greater than twice the level experienced in the previous five years. There is not necessarily a decrease in performance but potentially a misjudged increase in demand for assistance.

Is there a performance-related argument to alter the funding proposed for 2021?

- Since the funding projected for 2021 is the same amount as in the prior year, it appears reasonable to estimate a similar level of performance.
- If a higher probability for increased sites requesting assistance in 2021 over past years' experience is confirmed, the potential for increasing 2021 funding should be explored. If added funding is not possible, the denominator in the performance target for 2021 should be lowered to something more suitable to a sustained level of $38M in funding, as experienced in the previous year.

Appendix B: Multiple Program Area Analysis - Scatterplot

A scatterplot visualization, which displays performance and funding trends across multiple programs in a single exhibit, can provide an overview of the organization's performance. This approach is more compatible with the strategically-oriented perspectives of the senior leadership and management. They can review the representative funding and performance trends of several program areas across the organization on a single exhibit. From this review they can determine which program areas are most in need of further discussion. In a scatterplot visualization, trends in performance and funding for each program area cover multiple past years to be compared with targets for the next two future planning years. The following discusses the method for constructing such a scatterplot visualization, and suggestions for its use.

STEP 1: Calculate coordinates representing the performance and funding trends

Trends in performance and funding for each program area can be plotted on a scatterplot where the coordinates are calculated as depicted in Figure 16:

- X coordinate (funding trend index): the percentage change in the average annual program funding targeted for the present year and the next future year from the average actual program funding for the past 3-5 years.

- Y coordinate (performance trend index): the percentage change in the average annual performance targeted for the present year and the next future years from the average actual annual performance for the past 3-5 years. This change in the average annual performance (from past/actual performance to future/targeted performance) for the program area is represented as the sum of the changes calculated for each of the program area's key performance indicators.

These coordinates are calculated from the same performance and funding data that is already being collected for the organization's annual performance plan and annual performance report to help ensure continuity, attribution, and traceability. For performance measures expressed as percentages, using the numerators of the percentages in the measures is recommended in calculating the performance trend for the scatterplot. The numerator of the performance measure's percentage is considered to more closely represent the amount of the annual achievement relative to the amount of annual funding invested.

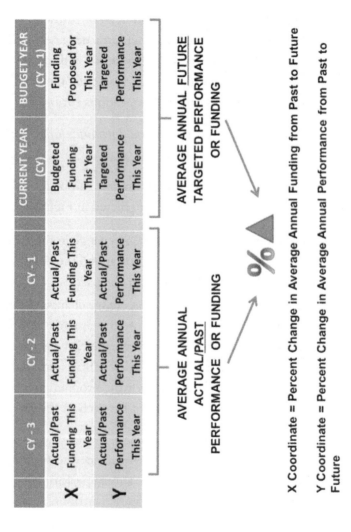

Figure 16. Calculating index values for coordinates on scatterplot

STEP 2: Plot coordinates representing the performance and funding trends of the multiple program areas on the scatterplot

The following copy of Figure 13 (from Chapter 6) displays the combined percentage change in performance and funding for each health program area (calculated from data in Table 5 using the method depicted in Figure 16). Executives and managers can focus their attention according to the following categorization of program areas based on their locations in the quadrants of the scatterplot, where:

- Located in either the upper left or upper right quadrant - not urgently in need of adjustment/action since "Increasing Performance with Decreasing Funding" is considered a desirable condition and "Increasing Performance with Increasing Funding" is typically an acceptable condition unless different from senior leadership and management's expectations;

- Located in lower left quadrant - potentially in need of further adjustment/action since "Decreasing Performance with Decreasing Funding" is considered an understandable condition, i.e., less funding likely to yield less performance, unless this is contrary to the organization leader's priorities and/or expectations;

- Located in the lower right quadrant - recommended for further review with higher potential for adjustment/action since "Decreasing Performance with Increasing Funding" is not intuitively readily acceptable without a reasonable explanation.

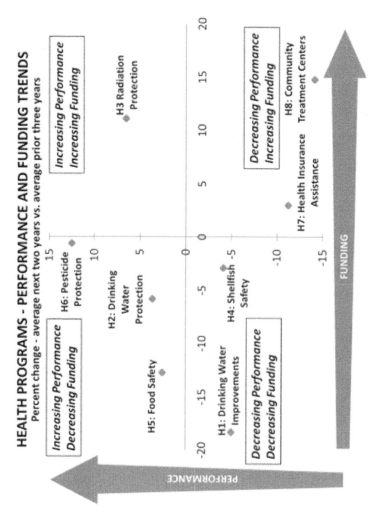

Figure 13. Performance and funding trends for multiple programs on a single display

STEP 3: Observations from the Scatterplot

The following illustrates how the scatterplot can be used to assess performance and funding across the organization and foster discussions that assist decision-making.

Categorize the program areas as follows depending upon the quadrant where they are located on the scatterplot.

Not urgently in need of adjustment/action - The program areas that are likely to not need additional attention in the planning process, as they are demonstrating favorable or acceptable performance and funding trends, are located in the upper two quadrants:

- Increasing performance and decreasing funding:
    o Drinking Water Protection (H2)
    o Food Safety (H5)
    o Pesticide Protection (H6)
- Increasing performance and increasing funding:
    o Radiation Protection (H3)

Potentially in need of further adjustment/action - Program areas that demonstrate both decreasing trends in performance and funding in the lower left quadrant appear intuitive; where less performance is likely to be achieved where there is less funding. However, if these program areas are of a higher priority, where an increase in future performance is desired over the presently planned levels, then the senior leadership and management may decide to add more funding or adjust activities to help increase future performance:

- Drinking Water Improvements (H1)
- Shellfish Safety (H4)

Recommended for further review with higher potential for adjustment/action - The decreasing performance and increasing funding quadrant identifies those program areas that are most in need of further review and potential adjustment or action to better ensure success. Data points plotted in the lower right quadrant reflect where targeted average annual performance is lower than the past realized average annual performance, while projected average annual funding is higher than that provided in the past:

- Health Insurance Assistance (H7)
- Community Treatment Centers (H8)

Consider possible positive and negative reasons for program areas being in the lower right quadrant, where the funding trend is increasing but the performance trend is decreasing. Demonstrating decreasing performance and increasing funding could indicate a deficiency in the program's execution or management requiring an alternate program approach and/or funding adjustment. But this is not necessarily a definite determination of poor performance. These trends could also indicate programs where:

- future performance may take several years to be realized beyond the increases in funding provided in the next two years;
- increasingly more challenging cases are being handled by the program that are in need of more funding than is being provided;
- future performance has been underestimated; or
- a performance indicator is inadequate in representing the program area.

These program areas in the lower right quadrant should be reviewed further to determine (1) if there are corrective actions needed to better ensure success or (2) if there has been a change in the program scope or complexity of projects that could slow performance relative to the increasing funding.

Potential changes to the budget should be considered, based on the relative position of program areas on the scatterplot.

Reconsider whether the level of funding for program areas in the lower right quadrant, where the funding trend is increasing but the performance trend is decreasing, should or should not be increased. If a weakness or deficiency in the management or implementation of these programs is found under further exploration, funding should not be increased and at least held constant until an increase in performance can be better assured. A need for additional funding could be justified if the reason for the decreasing performance is due to an increase in scope or complexity for which the presently planned increase in funding is still inadequate.

Consider whether additional funding should be added to any of the program areas in the lower left quadrant, which presently demonstrate decreasing performance with decreasing funding, if the program area is considered to need more work than had been presently planned.

Try to guard against inappropriate conclusions when using the scatterplot.

The position of program areas on the scatterplot might be misinterpreted as a reflection of their relative quality, value, or priority. Program areas above the X-axis could be mistaken to be higher priority or better performers than programs below the X-axis. Program areas below the X-axis could be misinterpreted as less important or poorer performers, leading to negative reactions from management, constituencies, overseers, or Congress, without the appropriate follow-up analysis or discussions that are meant to be encouraged by the scatterplot visualization.

In using the scatterplot, program areas displaying larger performance index values (i.e., larger changes in average annual performance) are not necessarily "better" performers than those with smaller or no changes in average annual performance. For example, while one program area might display a performance index value of +20%, that does not necessarily mean that its performance is twice "better" than another program area displaying a performance index of +10%.

A program area maintaining the same average annual level of performance will display a performance index value of 0% but that does not necessarily indicate that the program area is a poor performer. Maintaining the same level of performance can still be considered adequate, such as where an effective safety level, or a sustained level of performance despite worsening environmental conditions, is being maintained.

As it provides perspectives on performance and funding across different types of programs with differing levels of scope, complexity, and number of metrics, there is always the potential that a specific detail or program condition will be missed. However, the scatterplot visualization is a management tool meant to provide a more holistic perspective across a wide range of program areas helping performance information to be more useful at an executive or strategic level. It is important that the scatterplot visualization be used to facilitate selective exploration and discussion, rather than being assumed to provide an ultimate answer on the relative conditions of each individual program.

Table 5. Health program performance and funding data

		Actual CY-3	Actual Perf CY-2	Actual Perf CY-1	Target CY	Target CY+1	Funding Index	Performance Index
H1	Drinking Water System Improvement Projects	$200,000	$360,000	$288,000	$248,000	$214,000	-18.3%	-5.0%
	Percent of projects completed on time, as per contract (within scope of work)	65	65	91	70	70		-5.0%
H2	Drinking Water Protection	$16,000,000	$20,147,000	$18,245,000	$16,062,000	$18,095,000	-5.8%	3.6%
	Percent of drinking water inspections completed with no significant deficiencies	75	75	75	88	88		17.3%
	Percent of significant deficiencies addressed within 45 days of notification	60	60	64	55	55		-10.2%
H3	Community Radiation Protection	$12,000,000	$14,117,000	$13,906,000	$14,379,000	$15,278,000	11.1%	6.5%
	Percent of radiation inspections completed with no critical violations	90	90	88	95	95		6.5%
H4	Shellfish Food Safety	$3,423,000	$3,423,000	$3,306,000	$3,316,000	$3,259,000	-2.9%	-4.1%
	Number of acres of shellfish beds reopened that are currently closed to commercial and recreational harvest	100	100	1,422	500	500		-7.5%
	Percent of shellfish inspections completed with no critical violations	98	98	97	97	97		-0.7%
H5	Food Safety	$4,522,000	$4,522,000	$4,565,000	$3,946,000	$3,975,000	-12.7%	2.5%
	handlers, and food processing firms in compliance with public health and sanitation standards	93	93	92	95	95		2.5%
H6	Pesticide Protection / Regulation	$6,146,000	$6,146,000	$5,980,000	$6,044,000	$6,061,000	-0.6%	12.5%
	appropriate enforcement actions, completed within 160 days	94	94	80	100	100		12.5%
H7	Health Insurance Assistance	$2,466,000	$2,466,000	$2,706,000	$2,617,000	$2,628,000	3.0%	-11.2%
	and answered by the Office of the Insurance Commissioner	34,598	34,598	30,739	29,425	29,750		-11.2%
H8	Community Drug and Alcohol Treatment Centers	$81,364,000	$81,364,000	$82,142,000	$90,609,000	$96,847,000	14.8%	-14.1%
	Percent of prevention programs that represent evidence based, best or promising practice	69	69	72	60	60		-14.1%

Appendix C: Performance Management Analyst Competencies

Source: Memorandum from U.S. Office of Personnel Management Director to Federal Government Chief Human Capital Officers; <u>Government Performance and Results Act Modernization Act of 2010 Functional Competencies</u>; January 3, 2012.

Accountability	Holds self and others accountable for measurable high-quality, timely, and cost-effective results. Determines objectives, sets priorities, and delegates work. Accepts responsibility for mistakes. Complies with established control systems and rules.
Attention to Detail	Is thorough when performing work and conscientious about attending to detail.
Change Management	Knowledge of change management principles, strategies, and techniques required for effectively planning, implementing, and evaluating change in the organization.
Compliance	Knowledge of procedures for assessing, evaluating, and monitoring programs or projects for compliance with Federal laws, regulations, and guidance.
Conflict Management	Encourages creative tension and differences of opinions. Anticipates and takes steps to prevent counter-productive confrontations. Manages and resolves conflicts and disagreements in a constructive manner.

Creativity and Innovation	Develops new insights into situations; questions conventional approaches; encourages new ideas and innovations; designs and implements new or cutting-edge programs/processes.
Customer Service	Works with clients and customers (that is, any individuals who use or receive the services or products that your work unit produces, including the general public, individuals who work in the agency, other agencies, or organizations outside the Government) to assess their needs, provide information or assistance, resolve their problems, or satisfy their expectations; knows about available products and services; is committed to providing quality products and services.
Decision Making	Makes sound, well-informed, and objective decisions; perceives the impact and implications of decisions; commits to action, even in uncertain situations, to accomplish organizational goals; causes change.
External Awareness	Understands and keeps up-to-date on local, national, and international policies and trends that affect the organization and shape stakeholders' views; is aware of the organization's impact on the external environment.
Financial Analysis	Knowledge of the principles, methods, and techniques of financial analysis, forecasting, and modeling to interpret quantitative and qualitative data; includes data modeling, earned value management, and evaluating key financial indicators, trends, and historical data.

Flexibility	Is open to change and new information; rapidly adapts to new information, changing conditions, or unexpected obstacles.
Influencing/Negotiating	Persuades others; builds consensus through give and take; gains cooperation from others to obtain information and accomplish goals.
Information Management	Identifies a need for and knows where or how to gather information; organizes and maintains information or information management systems.
Interpersonal Skills	Shows understanding, friendliness, courtesy, tact, empathy, concern, and politeness to others; develops and maintains effective relationships with others; may include effectively dealing with individuals who are difficult, hostile, or distressed; relates well to people from varied backgrounds and different situations; is sensitive to cultural diversity, race, gender, disabilities, and other individual differences.
Leadership	Influences, motivates, and challenges others; adapts leadership styles to a variety of situations.
Legal, Government and Jurisprudence	Knowledge of laws, legal codes, court procedures, precedents, legal practices and documents, Government regulations, Executive orders, agency rules, Government organization and functions, and the democratic political process.
Mathematical Reasoning	Solves practical problems by choosing appropriately from a variety of mathematical and statistical techniques.

Oral Communication	Expresses information (for example, ideas or facts) to individuals or groups effectively, taking into account the audience and nature of the information (for example, technical, sensitive, controversial); makes clear and convincing oral presentations; listens to others, attends to nonverbal cues, and responds appropriately.
Organizational Awareness	Knows the organization's mission and functions, and how its social, political, and technological systems work and operates effectively within them; this includes the programs, policies, procedures, rules, and regulations of the organization.
Organizational Performance Analysis	Knowledge of the methods, techniques, and tools used to analyze program, organizational, and mission performance; includes methods that deliver key performance information (for example, comparative, trend, diagnostic, root cause, predictive) used to inform decisions, actions, communications, and accountability systems.
Partnering	Develops networks and builds alliances; collaborates across boundaries to build strategic relationships and achieve common goals.
Performance Measurement	Knowledge of the principles and methods for evaluating program or organizational performance using financial and nonfinancial measures, including identification of evaluation factors (for example, workload, personnel requirements), metrics, and outcomes.

Planning and Evaluating	Organizes work, sets priorities, and determines resource requirements; determines short- or long-term goals and strategies to achieve them; coordinates with other organizations or parts of the organization to accomplish goals; monitors progress and evaluates outcomes.
Political Savvy	Identifies the internal and external politics that impact the work of the organization. Perceives organizational and political reality and acts accordingly.
Problem Solving	Identifies and analyzes problems; weighs relevance and accuracy of information; generates and evaluates alternative solutions; makes recommendations.
Project Management	Knowledge of the principles, methods, or tools for developing, scheduling, coordinating, and managing projects and resources, including monitoring and inspecting costs, work, and contractor performance.
Reasoning	Identifies rules, principles, or relationships that explain facts, data, or other information; analyzes information and makes correct inferences or draws accurate conclusions.

Resilience	Deals effectively with pressure; remains optimistic and persistent, even under adversity. Recovers quickly from setbacks.
Strategic Thinking	Formulates objectives and priorities, and implements plans consistent with the long-term interests of the organization in a global environment. Capitalizes on opportunities and manages risks.
Team Building	Inspires and fosters team commitment, spirit, pride, and trust. Facilitates cooperation and motivates team members to accomplish group goals.
Technical Competence	Uses knowledge that is acquired through formal training or extensive on-the-job experience to perform one's job; works with, understands, and evaluates technical information related to the job; advises others on technical issues.
Technical Credibility	Understands and appropriately applies principles, procedures, requirements, regulations, and policies related to specialized expertise.
Vision	Takes a long-term view and builds a shared vision with others; acts as a catalyst for organizational change. Influences others to translate vision into action.
Written Communication	Writes in a clear, concise, organized, and convincing manner for the intended audience.

REFERENCES

AGA Association of Government Accountants Corporate Partner Advisory Group (2006). <u>PAR, The Report We Hate to Love</u> (p. 4). Alexandria, VA: AGA (Association of Government Accountants).

Beck, Richard T. (1993). Engagement: Promoting Intergroup Collaboration and Innovation in Effective Research and Development Management (Doctoral dissertation, George Mason University, 1993). <u>ProQuest Dissertations and Thesis Database</u>, 9323969.

Beck, Richard T. and O'Brien, John L. (2015, 2018, 2019). Applying Performance and Funding Trend Data: A Tool to Foster Dialogue Among Public Sector Leadership and Increase the Use of Performance Data. <u>Conference presentations</u>: New Jersey: Rutgers University; Washington, D.C.: American Society of Public Administration; Chicago: Midwest Political Science Association.

Fayol, Henri (1916). <u>Industrial and General Administration</u>.

Forrester, Jay W. (1968). <u>Principles of Systems</u> (pp. 3-5). Cambridge, Massachusetts: MIT Press.

Gulick, Luther (1937). Notes on the Theory of Organization. In Gulick, Luther H. & Urwick, L. (Ed.), <u>Papers on the Science of Administration</u> (pp. 3-45). New York: Columbia University Institute of Public Administration.

Kamensky, John M. (1993). Program Performance Measures: Designing a System to Manage for Results. <u>Public Productivity and Management Review</u>, <u>16</u>(4), 395-402.

Keegan, Michael J. (2015). <u>Perspective on the PerformanceStat Potential: A Leadership Strategy for Producing Results</u> (pp. 73-78). Washington, D.C.: IBM Center for the Business of Government.

Kohli, Jitinder (2010). <u>Golden Goals for Government Performance</u>. Washington, D.C.: Center for American Progress.

Lindblom, Charles (1959). The Science of "Muddling Through." <u>Public Administration Review, 19</u>(2), 79-88.

Lu, Yi (2008). Managing the Design of Performance Measures: The Role of Agencies. <u>Public Performance and Management Review, 32</u>(1), 7-24.

Simon, Herbert A. (1976). <u>Administrative Behavior (3rd Ed.)</u>, (p. 20-44). New York: The Free Press, Macmillan Publishing Company.

Solan, David (2009). The EPAStat Quarterly Report and Lessons Learned. <u>Public Performance and Management Review, 33</u>(2), 222-240.

U.S. Government Accountability Office (2018). <u>Managing for Results</u> (GAO-18-609SP). Washington, D.C., pp. 23-26.

U.S. Office of Management and Budget (2020). Agency Priority Goal information, on-line at <u>https://www.performance.gov/about/APG_about.html</u>. Washington, D.C.

U.S. Office of Management and Budget (2010). <u>Performance Improvement Guidance: Management Responsibilities and Government Performance and Results Act Documents</u>. Washington, D.C.: Memorandum M 10-24 from OMB Associate Director for Performance and Personnel Management.

U.S. Office of Personnel Management (2012). <u>Government Performance and Results Act Modernization Act of 2010 Functional Competencies</u>. Washington, D.C.: Memorandum from US Office of Personnel Management Director to Federal Government Chief Human Capital Officers (January 3, 2012).

U.S. Senate Committee on Homeland Security and Governmental Affairs (2009). <u>Getting to Better Government: Focusing on Performance</u> (September 23, 2009 hearing). Washington, D.C.: Subcommittee on Financial Management, Government Information, Federal Services, and International Security.

SUPPLEMENTAL RESOURCES

Barber, Michael (2008). Instruction to Deliver. London, England: Methuen.

Bryson, John M. (2018). Strategic Planning for Public and Nonprofit Organizations: A Guide to Strengthening and Sustaining Organizational Achievement. Hoboken, N.J.: John Wiley and Sons Inc.

Gessaman, Donald (2006). Understanding the Budget of the United States Government. Washington, D.C.: EOP Foundation.

Hatry, Harry P. and Wholey, Joseph S. (1999, 2006). Performance Measurement: Getting Results. Washington, D.C.: The Urban Institute Press.

W.K. Kellogg Foundation (2004). Logic Model Development Guide. Battle Creek, Michigan: W.K. Kellogg Foundation.

Long, E. and Franklin, A.L. (2004). The Paradox of Implementing the Government Performance and Results Act: Top–down Direction for Bottom–up Implementation. Public Administration Review, 64(3), 309-319.

Molyneux, Guy and Teixeira, Ruy, with Whaley, John (2010); Better Not Smaller - What Americans Want from Their Federal Government. Washington, D.C.: Center for American Progress.

Moynihan, Donald P (2008). The Dynamics of Performance Management: Constructing Information and Reform. Washington, D.C.: Georgetown University Press.

Poister, Theodore H., Aristigueta, Maria P., Hall, Jeremy L. (2015). Measuring Performance in Public and Nonprofit Organizations: An Integrated Approach (2nd Edition). San Francisco: Jossey-Bass, John Wiley and Sons Inc.

Sabatier, Paul A. (1986). Top-down and Bottom-up Approaches to Implementation Research: A Critical Analysis and Suggested Synthesis. Journal of Public Policy, 6(1), 21-48.